How to Survive Education

# How to Survive Education BEFORE, DURING, AND AFTER COLLEGE

Richard M. Gummere, Jr.

HARCOURT BRACE JOVANOVICH, INC.
NEW YORK

Some of the material in this book first appeared in
*The Guidance Point of View, Harper's Magazine,* and
*The Nation.* Chapter 3 is reprinted by permission
from *Lithopinion* #7, graphic arts and public affairs
journal of Local One, Amalgamated Lithographers of
America, New York (under the title "The Great
College Grab Bag").

ISBN 0-15-142178-1
*Library of Congress Catalog Card Number: 74-160402*
*Printed in the United States of America*
A B C D E

# Foreword

My ancestors have been scribbling away at books for a century and a half. Great-great-grandfather John, a scientist, college president, and father of eleven children, wrote two successful books. He also managed the college farm. Great-grandfather Samuel, another college president, wrote a long epic poem in the style of Byron's *Don Juan*. It described his trip across Iowa in the 1850's to observe the transit of Venus. Since then, off the family production line have come seven scholarly works by my grandfather (one just reissued), and an unsuccessful novel; three Quaker histories by my grandmother and an edition of John Woolman's *Journal*; five books by my father, two of them written during his eighties (an early one on Seneca has just been reissued); a fine travel book by Cousin Harry; and numerous Latin textbooks by Cousin Jack. Here comes my book.

How could I not have written it? I'd been comfortably turning out magazine articles about students and colleges, defending them against pessimistic critics. These were quoted here and there, pirated a bit, and one republished in Japanese. But three were republished in American college textbooks. So one day my agent, Marie Rodell, said I must put my ideas into a book of my own. A book! I exclaimed. How could I write a book? When would I write it?

Mrs. Rodell is gentle but inexorable. She reminded me that I'd told her of the family mania, passed down like the Bourbons' hemophilia. It was all over soon, and we were sitting with William B. Goodman, an editor of Harcourt Brace Jovanovich, to discuss an outline. His son was then a candidate for college. We had found a seasoned editor who was also a parent hungry for clues to the admissionary mysteries of the academic labyrinth—an ideal person to help me with the book.

The labyrinth itself may be more intricate today than ever. Many of us educators admit we are baffled by it, but also fascinated. Here may I offer some clues and try at the same time to convey the fascination of higher education? The facts sober us; the romance engages us.

To whom else should thanks go for special help in writing the book? To my children, who have done some valuable editing and put up with a preoccupied crackpot, and to my wife, Peg, who cleared, furnished, painted, and guarded my two studies. "Turn that hi-fi down! Pop's writing." Also, for her I might imitate the Bard College student's dedication: "To my advisor who, without my help, could not have written this Senior Project."

I must also thank three men for their example of early rising. My father-in-law, Elisha Mowry, aged eighty-nine, still gets up as early as 3 A.M. to do the endless work that has earned him a CBE from the Queen of England and the dedication of an edition of Cicero's work *On Old Age*. George Washington, of whom three portraits now hang on my bulletin board, rose at 4:30 A.M. He also went to bed at 9 P.M. sharp. If guests lingered, Martha would start easing them out around 8:55. (I just doze off in my chair.) And Hal Holbrook. Each day, I recall Mr. Holbrook's dedication of his re-creation of Mark Twain—an extraordinary achievement of art and scholarship—to the little birds who in the dawn hours cheered him.

Lastly, hundreds upon hundreds of college students, the largest number from Bard College and Columbia University, have talked with me candidly about themselves. They make me think of the disclaimer of the lion tamer to the circus manager who was writing out a check for his act: "Of course, I wouldn't be worth a quarter without them lions."

R.M.G., Jr.

*March 25, 1971*

# Contents

How to Survive Education

# Introduction: Backstage

*Man is only born ignorant. It takes four years of college to make him stupid.*                              —MARK TWAIN

I was born and raised on a college campus, and most of my life has been spent in a college environment. Closeness to the educational scene over many years has given me a backstage view of the props, familiarity with actors and stagehands, and —tempered by irreverence—devotion to the show.

Faculty children exploit the campus for all it's worth. During college vacations or weekends we could easily break into the chemistry laboratories and the astronomy observatory. The administration offices did not tempt us, but the engineering building and the powerhouse did. The gymnasium was a favorite target, with its scores of dumbbells, which we could roll across the basketball floor. If free cider was served at a student or faculty smoker, we got some. But we could also prey on an occasionally unattended refreshment stand in one of the dormitories. We were allowed to use the skating rink, the swimming pool, and the library. Again we preferred our own initiative: waiting until a bank between two athletic fields had been carefully graded and grassed, we improved it with a large dugout like those the American Doughboys were then constructing in France. To us, scholars appeared quite fallible: we heard them gossiped about by their neighbors, saw them scolded by their wives. The college's president, with whose children we played, did not impress us as much as the head gardener. Faculty could even appear ridiculous, like the historian next door who, at the news of the 1918 Armistice, threw his derby high in the air to see it land on his garage roof.

My lack of reverence for higher education is all the greater because I became a college student at a time when almost anybody could get in almost anywhere. I applied to Harvard in 1930. For slightly more than 1,000 places in the freshman class about 1,200 candidates applied. Of these, only 60 were turned down. That rejection rate bothered the Dean of Admissions so much that he wrote a memo about it to the President. Open admissions recently has been challenged as though it were an outrageous innovation. To me, it looks like the old days.

Were we all serious and successful students anyway? Hardly. Some were scholars. Though our studies would now be considered modest in scope and depth, a few worked at them long and late in order to graduate with high rank. But most of us reserved a day or two for shrewd study near the end of each term. To help make that stunt come off, we could choose among several cram schools in the neighborhood.

We put our best time and energy into pleasure. Typically this included much more of girls, liquor, sports, and miscellaneous trifling than can be seen on today's campuses. Even our sex life was lighthearted. I knew only one classmate who got married before graduation and only one who was engaged. We upset the local citizenry not by our protest but by our escapades. One night I rented a car with another senior (he now is a New York *Times* columnist). Discovering that the speedometer did not record mileage in reverse, we zigzagged backwards through the Boston suburbs, bringing a number of householders running out in alarm at the strange roar of our engine. Was my college exceptional? A unique island of undergraduate irresponsibility? Alumni of other schools recall the same sort of experience. Vincent Sheean described his fellow students a few years earlier at the University of Chicago as "two thousand nincompoops." Conscientious frivolity was the thing.

Looking at higher education without awe or sentimentality, I see a number of paradoxes. It trains some of the population to think; it gives more a trained incapacity to do so. It is supposed to breed leaders, and sometimes does. But it also breeds followers in hordes. It resists change, yet it is always changing. Our 23 million alumni save the society from hopeless parochialism, but their own inertia is one of our greatest dangers. Like the parliament, the university is one of the great inventions of modern Western man. Like the Spanish Inquisition, it could miscarry and end up a tragic memory.

# 1 / Function

*I came here for an experience, but all it seems to offer is preparation. And I don't know what it's preparing me for.*

—A COLLEGE SENIOR

The origin of formal education is obscure. But V. Gordon Childe, the archaeologist, describes art schools in the Upper Paleolithic time. Early hunters believed that if someone painted a woolly mammoth on the wall of their cave, they could catch one more easily, so they chose their best artists and put them in charge of classes in painting. To our hungry primitive kin, this work probably counted much more for its use than for its beauty.

Formal education has never lost this early emphasis on the utilitarian. It has prepared people to work and to serve the political purposes of society. In early Athens, children's schooling was concentrated on gymnastics, dance, and the memorizing and singing of Homer. Its aim was to breed an elite of

7

warriors and roving entrepreneurs. The more often a boy sang or played a lyre for a classmate who sang about those endless battles in front of Troy, or about Ulysses outmaneuvering everybody he met on his travels, the better imperialist that boy would grow up to be. Athenian schools, then, were serving a military-industrial complex like ours.

But after Athens lost her independence to the Macedonians, words rather than deeds became the vocation of the upper classes. A more intellectual type of higher study was invented, which survives today. Aristotle posed the problems and made the rules. He made them especially strict because of the fear of self-indulgence he acquired tutoring young Alexander of Macedon, a royal super-hipster, and observing his own fellow Athenians. They agreed, as Will Durant said, "that honesty is the best policy, but they tried everything else first." So Aristotle proved to us that we have reason; he invented logic to help us discipline it; he wrote a book on ethics; he taught us to study the world patiently, and to that end he divided it up into neat, convenient segments such as physics, metaphysics, rhetoric, grammar, biology, psychology, political science.

This curriculum was imported by the Romans. At the time, they, too, were declining politically under an autocrat. But they were also developing legal needs and skills. As the Empire spread and grew complicated, they had to have articulate lawyers to organize and justify it. So their schools, too, focused on words. Typical faculty are said to have been misfits. A large proportion were slaves. But their skill in training talkers was highly valued. A slave who was a top grammarian might be sold on the Roman market for as much as a top major-league athlete today. Quintilian, the most renowned Roman educator, was quite clear about the chief purpose of imperial schools: to prepare orators. The Greeks had developed these studies to fill up the time. The Romans used them in addition for professional training. They named them the liberal arts, from the adjective *liberalis:* "becoming to a free man." Development of the brain and the tongue was not for a slave, except to teach. Otherwise, he was supposed to be building an aqueduct.

Our early-American college educators turned the liberal arts curriculum, again, to the taming of barbarians. Our colonial population tended to act like Goths. They needed tough discipline. So to the fear of hell-fire in religion the educators added tough Aristotelian discipline in schooling. A large proportion of our early graduates became clergymen. And on the seal of seventeenth-century Harvard the goal of the system was expressed in one word: *Veritas.* That did not mean objective truth. It meant nearly the opposite, that is, religious truth as the Puritans wanted to enforce it. And enforce it they did. One of their earliest and best college presidents had to resign because he opposed the baptism of children. They even hanged an ancestor of mine, among others, for refusing to give up his Quaker beliefs.

Until after the Civil War, everything in the college program was religious discipline for young savages: the Latin and Greek and mathematics toughened their character, the science awed them with the marvels of God's creation, the theological studies and exercises—backed up by at least fourteen chapel services per week—prepared their souls for the next world. Not at all in sarcasm were our early nineteenth-century colleges called "Schools of Prophets." Faculty tried to keep the campus tense with religious anxiety. This would flare up in revivals, often several days long, at which various professors led prayers, and students by the hundreds threw away their hidden brandy bottles and playing cards and accepted Christ. Even Princeton, whose annals boast the brief presidency of Jonathan Edwards, was described by one of her early nineteenth-century trustees as a "Temple of Piety," and a revival is recorded there as late as the 1880's.

Today, the liberal arts studies have been turned from those pious purposes. Instead of saving souls, they are now used to process middle-class, middle-brow, middle-management experts. For this purpose, scholars and teachers have calmed down. Instead of a religious trip, they offer a young person a training program.

To turn out graduates who are articulate, predictable, adroit, busy, patient, and sedentary, our colleges and universities have developed an elaborate system of quizzes and exams to be maneuvered through, deadlines to be met—a little frantically —marks to be racked up, course credits to be accumulated in a pattern acceptable to the Registrar, professors to be psyched, and peers to be outsmarted in the classroom competition. Extracurricular activities, too, have prepared young people for middle-level corporate work. A varsity team, the Lit, a dorm council, freshman orientation, Young Democrats, and whatever, help train reliable doers. After graduation, many are ready to operate the "Clean Machine"—as bureaucrats to do routine, as technocrats to plan, as meritocrats to manage.

Education for those tasks needs a narrow focus. It was described by McGeorge Bundy, former Dean of Harvard, White House staffer, and now President of the Ford Foundation, in a recent article in the scholars' quarterly *Daedalus*. He admits that faculty shortcomings did contribute to our campus troubles. But he defends the faculty's dedication to training the mind only:

We were absolutely right about one vital point; we knew what the university was for: learning. The university is for learning—not for politics, not for growing up, not even for virtue, except as these things cut in and out of learning and except as they are necessary elements of all good human activity.

Bundy's frankly narrow view of learning has been spreading for about 100 years. It came in with modern science. It fits the stereotype of the scientist—cold, professional, insular. Cold? Imagine a laboratory wizard synthesizing protoplasm or smashing atoms. According to the complaints of many students, that is how too many instructors try to appear. They won't even show their real feelings about scholarly issues, let alone about other issues. "Most think that's bad taste, like a confession in any encounter session." Professional? A young scholar can earn a Ph.D. in history or physics without ever hearing any discussion of their uses except as they provide an occupation for historians and physicists. Asked which of his students he would recommend for a fellowship at a polar- and space-research station in Antarctica, the chairman of a physics department replied, "None of them. That would only interrupt their academic careers." He had forgotten about Darwin's stay among the finches, turtles, and lizards of the Galápagos Archipelago. Insular? The scientific model encourages strict specialism. Even in a small Midwestern denominational college, I heard an economics professor declare, "All I want to do with any student of mine is to make him into a good economist." This sort of education expressed well enough the style of a society reckless of people but devoted to processes and things. Our irresponsible, selfish education fits that materialism. What sort of education will fit the humanitarianism that man must now substitute for the materialism if survival is to be both possible and sweet?

# 2 / Irony

*"What would you do if I sang out of tune?" sang the Beatles, out of tune.*

"The design of our system of higher education is intricate, like a Scotch plaid; its pattern keeps shifting, like a kaleidoscope; its major changes come slowly, like a glacier; and its flavor is bittersweet." This was the opening sentence of an earlier version of this book.

A college student read it and pronounced it too slick. Another made the same objection to other, similar passages elsewhere in the book. Leave off the varnish, they said. Don't put a smooth finish over a rough story. Hiding the truth? Escaping it?

I was once a Latin teacher, and early in my classical training I fell under the influence of the glorious periodic sentences of Cicero and the elegant hexameters of Virgil, "wielder of the stateliest measure ever moulded by the lips of man." But can today's college scene possibly be described in graceful, neoclassical prose?

Higher education has improved since I was a student. The teaching is better, the curriculum richer, the students busier, more mature. But it's not prettier. It never was as pretty as they said. Today, its features are darkening with anxiety.

My neoclassical style might serve well to describe the sound of Founders' Bell floating over wide lawns, but what about the tedium of being lectured at? This book is an attempt to put together a collage of a student's experience: his hysteria in the stadium during a close game, his suspicion that he went to the wrong college, his delight in going out at 3 A.M. for a sandwich, his frustration at finding himself working only for marks. Old Professor Smith's annual lecture on Garibaldi in History 3402 (standing room only) must be included in the collage—along with the nearly unbearable noise of freshmen in the dorm. The camaraderie in the car pool must somehow be balanced against the cold shoulder a commuter gets from the residential students. Can I use stately sentences to describe the peculiar experience of a certain student who rode the subway for an hour and a half each way to and from the College of the City of New York? An ordeal? On the contrary. No interruptions, the serenity of reading science and humanities against the roar of the express, the calisthenics of the lurching car; never studied as well or enjoyably before. T. S. Eliot had a phrase: "The horror, boredom, and glory of it all."

The studied dishevelment of the students will probably be a surprise to many, perhaps especially to parents, who risk a visit to campus. It's not new. In the mid-1950's, the headmaster of a fashionable private school went to see his recent graduates at a fashionable men's college. They ate together in the stately Gothic dining hall. But his old boys were dressed like hobos, he lamented, or like a pirate crew. He begged them to look up at the beautiful vaulting, then at their sweat shirts and sneakers. How could they bear the incongruity? Today, a couple of them probably would have come in bare feet. And at about that time, the college adviser of a public high school got a phone call from a couple of alumni who were now at Haverford College. Did he know how they could rent an elephant? Rent an elephant! What for? To parade around a striped tent that had been put up for the 125th anniversary celebration of the college. They had raised over $100 for the elephant but hadn't found one yet. The anniversary was all phony, they said, so why not make a real circus out of it?

Last fall I went to an educators' conference at a medium-sized college in rural Long Island. It was a warm October day. Some of the young men were going to class without any shirts. Our varsity athletes have been held by their coaches to conventional grooming—during the season. I know a sophomore who succeeded in kicking seventeen out of twenty touchdown conversions for Columbia last fall. He now wears a beard.

One parent discovered that younger faculty are changing style, too. At the end of the first term at a small, seasoned liberal arts college in the upper Midwest, a freshman, calling home over the long-distance phone, reported an *F*. Construing too literally a professor's general assurance that his lectures were to be attended only if they proved helpful and interesting, he had attended almost none. When he handed in his term paper a week late, the professor refused to read it. "What did your adviser say?" "He said, 'Fuck that bastard!' " The father was appalled at the professor's punitive thrust at his son and indignant at the adviser's crude response. So much, he thought, for sanctuaries of liberal decorum these days. "Well," he said, helplessly communicative, "you tell your adviser your father says to button his fuckin' lip."

The dissatisfaction with traditional style was revealed at the Columbia banquet of welcome for freshmen, September, 1970. Seven hundred of them were wearing jackets, ties, and even vests, many for the last time on campus. Beards were still scarce but hair plentiful and frequently at seventeenth-century shoulder length. Caterers, candles, linen tablecloths, grapefruit cup with maraschino cherries. Before speeches from the President and the Dean, the Glee Club sang a medley of college songs. Polished singing—tight, virile, fast. Hearty applause. The leader got a big laugh when he raised his baton to conduct a student drinking song, which they were only offering, he explained over his shoulder, because they had no smoking song.

Then the college's alma-mater hymn, *"Sans Souci"*—"Free of Care"—a gem of late-nineteenth-century collegiate romance. College is hailed as a warm haven from a tough world, the "bright years" of the undergraduate a last chance for exuberant fellowship. The harmony had been slightly rearranged, I suspect, to point up the ironic blend in mood of gaiety and melancholy. The men of the Glee Club sang perfectly. Too perfectly. The irony was unbearable. The melodious song could not hold up under the sense of ambiguity about education even in still sanguine freshmen. Those old collegians gloried in irresponsibility. The new ones wondered if they were supposed to also. At first, the freshmen felt incredulous, then they grew concerned, finally they laughed uneasily.

The Dean, a warm and witty man, delivered a speech, scholarly enough for an introduction to four years at a distinguished liberal arts college and gay enough to fit the tone set by our mint parfait, *gâteaux*, and coffee. A few freshmen had lit up cigars. The Dean said he hoped they had come to take part in the old, difficult enterprise of clearer thinking, better ideas, and some little originality—as rare on a campus as anywhere. Indeed, H. L. Mencken may have been right in his estimate that the total of real thinking in the career of Aristotle himself added up to half an hour.

The Dean's audience seemed attentive as he went on to complain that the campus revolutionaries take enough risks but not enough thought. Maybe they're following a principle stated by George Bernard Shaw: that martyrdom is the only way to become famous without ability. But the campus revolution will succeed and lead to better education only if its members examine their goals and methods with the intellectual honesty that is the main concern of a liberal college.

The next day, when I asked one of the freshman for his reaction, he said he'd turned off. So had a couple of others. The Dean's an excellent man, they insisted. His remarks were quite appropriate for the event. And yet. Well. "There's so much else to think about when you've just gotten here." I believe these young men were indicating that they do not like the kind of grace with which my generation tries to clothe its thoughts.

Such grace marked the leadership of the chairman of a panel at a campus conference on "Alternative Careers." A middle-aged man in a suit, he looked strange in a roomful of young people seeking information about how to live and work apart from the corporate system. Yet he led the discussion with unusual tact as the panelists described and analyzed communes and new life styles, or as others aired their frustration at being victimized by a commercial society. He gave the floor often enough to the talkers, while drawing out the bashful. He knew how to enhance the balance, the shape of the give-and-take. He used humor. He helped the group develop warmth.

Some of the radicals there were put off by his success. Toward the end of the evening, they confronted him: the discussion had been smooth but not vital; he was condescending; and he was funny but not humorous; the warmth people felt was artificial; they couldn't believe that because he wore a beard he was liberated; it was an outcome of his finesse, not a flow from his or their hearts. Again the young people were reacting against a polish of which they were suspicious. "Don't you see?" someone explained to him afterwards. "It was too nice an evening." They thought it should be rougher—like the world.

But the grace they resent the most is that which we borrow from them, like the style of dress of the young people, which the clothes designers have borrowed and commercialized. A college woman used to visit the College Shoppe of a posh department store every August for her campus wardrobe. Now she sees her clothes in a boutique tagged with famous names and bought by suburban matrons. The long dresses that young women of "the Movement" recently put on to express nostalgia for a past they think was lovely are now being worn by the wealthy and the worldly for chic. But trust the rebels—many simply do an end run around the stylists to thrift shops where some are tatting genuine old garments for them at a reasonable price.

A beautiful horse by Marino Marini stands in the permanent collection of the Museum of Modern Art in New York City. Like the rusted metal and dented surfaces of much contemporary sculpture, the wood of this piece is rough, worm-holed, and a bit sprung at some of the seams. Marini's horse is deliberately crude in execution.

Why do young people today reject the finish that their elders have prized? Of all the reasons they give, I believe the most important one is this: they think it symbolizes our hypocrisy; they think we have used it to help ourselves overlook the unconscionable failures of our society; they think if we make the surface gleam brightly enough, we can't see through it so easily to the ugliness beneath.

# 3 / Sheepskin Curtain

*No one else in my family has ever gone to college. And they've tried to discourage me. But when I was small, I stood in front of the university chapel and saw four students pile out into the night singing Bach at the top of their lungs.*

*Then about that time, someone showed me around the Medical School, and I saw a fetus and a skeleton and a cross section of the human head.*     —GALYA LAWSON

Every June, when the students had gone home, the janitors cleaned up after them and threw out of the windows things that had been left behind. We campus urchins hovered around the dorms like sharks around a lifeboat. I remember the loot of one June cleaning day: a World War One howitzer shell, a trombone mouthpiece, and a small brass elephant. Though loaded with these, I could still dash for a blue object floating down and grab it first: a Yale banner! I marched proudly home and hung it over my bed, and from then until my senior year of high school I was determined to go to Yale.

But in the end, I put away the blue banner and went to a college that had been attended by my ancestors and was supposed to be scholarly. Yale was more renowned then for its

Muscular Christianity. Before settling down to the life of a philosopher, maybe I had attempted through my Yale fantasy to feel for a while like a Bulldog.

Tradition and whimsy still seem to influence many candidates. Some may make their choice like the fellow who attended Boston University because he caught a hockey puck fired into the stands by a BU player. Others may join the "March of the Lemmings," as George Grenville Benedict, once college adviser at Andover, called the flocking of his preppies to what they and their parents consider appropriately fashionable colleges. High school counselors may struggle to interest their seniors in a careful search. Dr. Abraham Lass, in his book *How to Prepare for College*, or John C. Hoy, in *Choosing a College*, may try to convince them that careful inquiry will help them find one where they will "fit." Dean Eugene Wilson and Professor Charles A. Bucher, in *College Ahead*, may try to teach them not only how to fit, but also how to cope with the unexpected—as in a moon landing. Meanwhile, young people remain satisfied to know astonishingly little about their future college. The choice made by typical students will be subject to geography, misinformation, and the inherent ambiguity of the higher-education system.

Geography? Most young Americans must attend a nearby college and make the most of it. An upstate Pennsylvania girl walked several miles to enroll in Wilkes College and study philosophy. She then went to the Placement Office to ask for a job. When the Director inquired about her financial resources, she held out her hand and showed him twenty-one cents.

Two astronomers interested in admissions demonstrated that even nationally known colleges attract most of their students according to geography. A college's pull on students could be measured by an equation made up of (1) the number of miles between the students' homes and the campus, (2) the population of the students' home state, and (3) the college's enrollment. It is strikingly similar to Isaac Newton's equation for the pull of gravity. In place of Newton's constant, put the number of that college's living alumni.

The astronomers contended that the Iron Law which their calculations expressed could be checked at the Registrar's Office of the colleges they studied. One was Vassar. Suppose the equation suggests there should be 11.43 St. Louisans now at Vassar. "How many students do you have from St. Louis?" you ask the Registrar. He looks it up. "Thirteen," he answers, or "Ten," or maybe "Eleven"—anyway, your figure will be a near enough miss.

Some sophisticated candidates seem to defy this Law of Geographical Attraction and obey the following rule: apply only to colleges near the East or West coasts—either Swarthmore or Stanford, Bowdoin or Pomona, the University of Pittsburgh or Berkeley—nothing in between. These seaboard snobs suppose that except for a few gems gleaming out of the Midwestern night—like Carleton, Grinnell, or St. Olaf's—the colleges between the Appalachians and the Rockies are attended only by raw provincials. A student from Bard spent his winter field period visiting some Midwestern campuses. To the astonishment of his friends, he came back with an enthusiastic account of De Pauw University in Indiana: many students with intellectual curiosity, respect for individuality, liberal views, and other Eastern accomplishments. His incredulous Eastern friends thought he should have encountered "a bunch of Babbitts."

But transfer students—several hundred thousand each year—neatly confirm the Law: many of these start out at a distant college imagining they will find a quiet life among the old elms on its hilltop or a lively one in its metropolis. And they do—for a year or two. Then the college authorities begin to seem more and more like their parents, fellow students like old high school friends, and the exotic environment like everywhere else. So they transfer back to an acceptable institution near home and relax into old ways. Rather than obeying geographical laws, following family or neighborhood myths, or trying to discover—as a high school student put it—"whether or not a college admits dogs," why don't more candidates and their parents also try to find out what colleges are really like? Exactly what is meant by Earlham's Japanese semester, Santa Cruz's humanities college, or Bard's environmental center?

Misinformation? Colleges are not trying any harder to give a candid picture of themselves than their prospective students are to get one. Frank Bowles, when President of the College Entrance Examination Board, called the publicity of higher education, especially the catalogue, "the dullest and least informative literature on earth." I can endorse this comment because I wrote a catalogue and several brochures for a college. I recall that I wanted to insert some description of the institution as I thought the students saw it. The President sternly forbade me to do so. Instead, he required me to rely entirely on the generalities through which the landscape of higher education is officially viewed as though through a downpour of rain.

Candidates and their parents are also at the mercy of journalists, who—after all—are occupationally trained to make the complex appear simple. *Life* magazine published a tour de force by a professional writer, Gerald Moore, who had been allowed to spend several weeks living in a dorm at Indiana University. "A Surprising Report," the editors entitled his attempt to describe its students, the surprise being Moore's discovery that they did not fit the platitudes about them fabricated by fellow journalists. But Moore only fell back on another platitude: that Indiana University students are "apathetic," a term applied by the old to the young when the young put their energies into things the old don't approve of or perhaps even see. In the letter columns of *Life* an Indiana University coed retorted that Moore's article was the "biggest laugh we've had in a long time. It is truly a shame that in his weeks on our campus he missed IU entirely."

At least the journalists are readable, like the late David Boroff, in his nine virtuoso characterizations of a sample of colleges and universities. For these sketches, published in his book, *Campus U.S.A.*, Boroff spent enough time on each campus and was alert enough to observe that a college is difficult to describe neatly. He still felt he had to try. So neat images emerge from his sketches of "Imperial Harvard," "Smith —The College for All-Around Girls," "Birmingham-Southern —The Genteel Tradition on a Southern Campus."

Most readable, interesting, and helpful of all education journalism was *Moderator*, the intercollegiate student magazine published at the University of Pennsylvania's Annenberg School of Communications. Yet even *Moderator* attempted naïve, global college characterizations in its monthly GLOF ("General Lack of Fiber") Awards to institutions the editors judged strikingly undistinguished. The first GLOF Award went to Parsons College, since discredited by academic officialdom, too. But the second went to Syracuse—a university, like any other large one, with far too many strengths among its weaknesses for so sweeping a judgment. The President of Syracuse's Student Senate answered *Moderator* with the best defense: irony. In the GLOF Award citation, Syracuse was blamed for accepting an endowment from a wealthy friend to provide ice cream at every meal, in perpetuity. "I am informed by the Syracuse University Food Service," the Student-Senate President retorted, "that at no meal is ice cream the *only* dessert offered. Pies and cakes are baked and served daily by the Syracuse University Bakeshop on campus, which, incidentally, bakes the best pies in Syracuse." *Moderator's* next GLOF Award went to the Miss America Beauty Pageant.

Not so readable and in the end no more helpful to applicants have been the experts in the study of higher education—a would-be science that became fashionable at about the same time as space navigation. The College Characteristics Index was an early accomplishment of this movement. A number of other, similar scales or inventories for describing colleges have been attempted. Sophisticated scholars have labored in less structured study of them at several specialized institutes. But their labors have not substantially helped prospective students. Although many institutions have now been characterized by some objective method—early ones were Chicago, Brooklyn, Syracuse, Colgate, and Michigan State—the results have not been made widely and easily available to candidates. As far as I know, only Antioch College has published any of its College Characteristics Index profile in its catalogue. Do educators hold back out of scientific scruples about the accuracy of these portraits? Or because the colleges are bashful? Do they fear flak like the letter from the Indiana University coed? Is the dose too strong? Or not strong enough?

Are students good at characterizing their own college? Yes and no. They know too much about it. They are too busy panning it with each other, whitewashing it with outsiders, or telling an official or semiofficial investigator whatever they think he wants to hear about it. And they make up images of other colleges rather too cavalierly. *Where the Girls Are*, a handbook put out a few years ago by the *Daily Princetonian* on the varieties and habits of women of 125 colleges, offered college characterizations—always amusing, often interesting, but focused on social life—which are admittedly stereotypes. The editors insisted they can be useful nevertheless. Judge for yourself:

Mount Holyoke girls, in case you didn't know, are bright. They provide a refreshing change from the all-too-frequent women's college dichotomy: low intelligence-purple eyelashes vs. high intelligence-purple prose. They are smart, but they don't try to knock you over by summarizing Western culture in just under five minutes; they can be social, but they won't try to tell you that only Chicago people save Long Island deb parties from being a complete drag. Mount Holyoke girls are great—just ask them.

Not surprisingly, the girls retaliated—in *Where the Boys Are*, by the *Mount Holyoke News* and the Smith College *Sophian*. Among ten Eastern men's colleges, Princeton is introduced as "the only place in the world where when a boy and his date walk past a mirror, it's the boy who stops to comb his hair."

Since then, *The Insider's Guide to the Colleges*, put out by the staff of the *Yale Daily News*, has offered characterizations of 230 colleges for both sexes, which are just as amusing as the *Daily Princetonian*'s, richer in significant facts, and more reassuring. Does this reflect a more sanguine spirit in the Bulldog than in the Tiger, or a widespread improvement in higher education in the last few years?

Without knowing it, college students do level with candidates through the senior-class yearbooks, which some admissions officers—at Union, Williams, Allegheny, Alderson-Broaddus, and many others—have been sending to high school guidance offices. High school counselors say these have been surprisingly popular. No surprise, really: stifled by the artificiality of official promotional literature, the candidates feel reassured to have in their hands the work of real college students. I suspect they even enjoy the individual pictures and biographies of the graduating college seniors, who look so different from the paragons usually shown in admissions literature. In spite of the efforts of the official yearbook photographer, many of them look homely enough to be real.

To be sure, yearbooks have been usually planned and written according to rigid conventions. But most include a large number of photographs the Public Relations Office would have suppressed: students asleep in class, drunk, kissing a girl good night, borrowing a buck, cheating in an exam, putting the college paper to bed at 4:30 A.M., speeding in an Alfa Romeo to a tryst on a distant campus.

A new type of yearbook is emerging—less traditional, more candid about college life, revealing even more of the unmentionable realities such as drugs, shacking-up, political protest. Will it continue to be sent to high school counselors' offices? The article about DePauw University in *The Insider's Guide* suggests not.

Last year, for example, the yearbook staff broke tradition and published a sharp and biting commentary on life at DePauw. The book shook more than a few people up, including the admissions office, which had ordered eighty-five copies. Upon seeing it, they decided it wasn't the mirror of "Good Ol' DePauw, rah, rah" that they wanted to help their recruiting efforts, and they tried (unsuccessfully) to get their money back.

Candidates and their parents are at the mercy, lastly, of the guidance profession. The best counselors can only gather up for them a modicum of available and useful data about colleges and lead them to it, like the proverbial horse, wistfully hoping they will drink; try to advise them about some admissions matters not so obvious that they can't miss them, *i.e.*, don't go to the University of Chicago if you don't test easily; try to convey to them—mostly in vain—that for most young people any college will be a shattering surprise and for a year or so an ordeal, and that at any college (within reason), if they try, they can find enough fine teachers and congenial students.

Several high school counselors hereabouts with whom I checked just now have not discovered or do not recommend *The Insider's Guide* or the more recent *Underground Guide to College* by Susan Berman. "I won't say that's a good book," one of them told me, "but our students have been latching onto it." That's why I can't evaluate it here: for several months, all the copies coming into my local bookstores get latched onto before I show up. Two counselors say they push free admissions literature sent by Prudential Insurance, Minnesota Mining and Manufacturing, and the New York *Daily News*.

Not surprisingly, a study revealed that even experienced counselors have substantial information about very few colleges. Too many of them presume on this skewed sample to give Godlike advice. One consequence is that a large proportion of the students I meet do not think their counselors helped them much, if at all.

Inherent ambiguity? Professor David Riesman, Harvard's educational sociologist, offers a clue to our society's hesitation to explore these admissions riddles more carefully: among its other functions in our culture, he suggests, higher education serves as a "rite of passage," a ceremony to introduce adolescents into adult society. Such a rite can be only solemn, or it can be threatening, or it can be highly dangerous—as when those young jungle initiates plunge headfirst from a high platform, to be barely saved by a vine rope from breaking their necks. But the rite must be nonsense, and—especially—it *must* be clothed in mystery.

College, then, is our complicated equivalent for that ritual sequestration of American Indian boys and girls for a few weeks to fast, converse with spirits, and perfect the hocus-pocus they would use in their initiation ceremony. In our advanced society we must sequester the young in a longer and even more unnatural trial. Beyond the money we spend on it today, we adults must also invest the experience with plenty of anxiety as well as ambiguity, and to delude the young, we must try to delude ourselves. So if some troublemaker tries to see what's really going on in higher education and broadcast his findings, shouldn't we take him—as the Woomagansetts took anyone who peeked inside their Hahowawa and told about what he saw there—and stake him out on an anthill?

Professor Riesman is probably right. But the Sheepskin Curtain may also be hung between us and an even more awesome mystery: colleges and universities are like Proteus, the slippery fellow in the fable. If you ever got a grip on him, he turned into something else and slid away. Maybe we cannot pin down and simplify usefully so complex a thing as an educational institution.

I remember the time when a college president or dean—especially if addressing either the freshmen or the alumni—would refer grandly to the purpose of his institution as the making of "The Minnesota Man" or "The Wellesley Woman"—creatures as imaginary as the phoenix or the griffin. When these monsters disappeared from our academic verbiage, another took their place—"The Well-rounded Person." President William Fels, of Bennington College, in his satirical article "Modern College Usage," pointed out that the phrase was heard only at men's colleges because "women do not like to think of themselves as spheres." Fels went on to offer a mathematical solution, using the formula for the area of a sphere—$4\pi r^2$—to help admissions committees identify well-rounded men.

But educators have since decided that these types make dull colleges. Instead, they say they will now try to gather together well-rounded student bodies. Not long ago the New York *Times* reported that some Ivy League admissions officers had just discovered how. Geographical distribution used to be their favorite means; now they have turned to socioeconomic distribution: admitting rough diamonds from across the tracks ahead of polished ones from across the continent.

It's not an accident that the new discovery still justifies the admission of a disadvantaged Negro or a neurotic oboist as well as an heir to great wealth or a chap of not too subtle culture with an effective knuckle ball. This search for what one Ivy League admissions officer called "greatness" has lowered the proportion of his freshmen admitted from privileged independent schools and raised it from public schools. This is hard on the Ivy-oriented independent schools, but the trend toward an ever richer mix will help keep the American college lively—and hard, if not impossible, to describe.

The Harvard *Crimson* now and then prints an unusually careful study of another college. When the editors wanted to describe Radcliffe, their writer (a "Cliffie") found not one type, but three. Her title was "The Three Flavors of Radcliffe," *i.e.*, Peach, Chocolate, and Lime. Around Cambridge, you might pick out the Peach by her cashmere sweater, the Chocolate by her work with the neighborhood poor, and the Lime by her heavy eye shadow and volume of Kierkegaard.

But the *Crimson* journalist's unusual thesis was this: none of the three represents Radcliffe.

The University of Virginia is firmly typed—at least up North —as a collection of genteel playboys. ("He's not drunk; I saw him move.") But one UVA student sent me some issues of a magazine he helped edit, which then was running a monthly contest for the best *haiku* poems. Obviously his university harbored a sizable number of poets in the midst of its prodigals.

Antioch College students were characterized by a writer in a *Holiday* magazine article as disheveled dissenters. He reluctantly mentioned that some conventional young people can be seen there: "Business and engineering majors playing softball behind the Science Building and do-good Community Government fanatics." But a friend of mine who taught at Antioch for a year as a visiting professor was struck mainly by the number and influence of those conventional students. He thought the vitality of Antioch's community depended on both types.

Columbia College is widely believed to attract mostly metropolitan go-getters. Our premeds, regarded even on campus as a Philistine lot (they aren't, really), do often come from New York City high schools. But in number and impact on college life, they are easily matched by fraternity Greeks, a cosmopolitan and decidedly epicurean lot. Add to these the activists and the aesthetes, the band and the rugby association, the theater gang, the sailing club, and the gourmet society. Add those who do nothing but study and those whose only distinction is that they do not even do that. Add the Afro-American

Society, who have founded two fraternities. Then try to fabricate an image of Columbia that would include all these splinter groups and eccentrics.

Many student poets would have more fun publishing *haiku* at Virginia, where there are unpoetic squares to be edified, than at Sarah Lawrence College, where there are poets to be socialized, and many 4-H'ers would have more fun rubbing elbows with sandaled existentialists at Antioch than with a solid constituency of young evangelicals at George Williams College. Columbia's Leftists, a couple of hundred strong, were happier picketing the U.S. Marine recruiters because they were jeered at by Columbia's own Rightists, also a couple of hundred strong, segregated by the Dean behind a hedge. In fact, all campus enthusiasts at Columbia must have at least secretly appreciated our Society of Mockery, which used to rally near any demonstration to carry placards and distribute leaflets—with nothing on them.

In each of ourselves lurks an antiself that feeds on opposition. Enough of that would not be provided in a college that really lived up to an image.

Fortunately, whatever types of people a college student seeks to cultivate, he can surely find them. On any campus in the country is a marvelous assemblage, including most of these oddities: good-time Charleys and grinds, busybodies and recluses, custom-car buffs, bridge players, hayseeds, hippies, fashion plates, salvationists, aesthetes, spendthrifts and misers, snobs and Caspar Milquetoasts, members of SDS and of Junior Kiwanis, stamp collectors, bird watchers, and perhaps one fellow whose passion is volcanoes and another the history of municipal street railways. I even knew a student who was a connoisseur of high-speed electric trolleys in the Southwest. "I used to risk my life," I boasted to him, "on the P & W's one-car Liberty-Bell Limited. It careened from Philadelphia to Allentown, Pennsylvania, with only two stops, sometimes, they say, hitting ninety miles an hour." "Did you say ninety?"

So we keep college candidates vague, if not misinformed. "Why did you go to Amherst, Chris?" "Oh, my mother went to Holyoke, ten miles away from it, and she said it was a

good college." "What led you to apply to Wagner, Tim?"
"Nothing really, except that I saw a football game there once."
"Did you have a good idea, Tammy, what Bryn Mawr would
be like?" "Not the slightest. My Uncle Charley simply assured
me Quaker education is the best." "What was your image of
Radcliffe, Sheila?" "None. I grew up in the next town, but
absolutely the only thing I knew about Radcliffe was the
Choral Society." "I applied to three colleges: Rutgers because
it's famous and near, Florida State because it's in Florida, and
Northeastern University because of the co-op program. No,
I didn't know a thing about Northeastern, except work-study
sounded good." "Why Harvard, Pat?" "Well, I assumed—
wrongly—it'd make me tweedy, like my school crew coach."
Said a blind candidate, "When a student guide showed me
around Columbia, I decided because all the turns in the paths
were right angles the college must be square."

# 4 / Riverbank Village

*The only sign of life in Pokeville was the smoke coming out of the crematory chimney.*

—Opening title, one-reel comedy, early 1920's

I often return to my old homestead near a mid-Hudson Valley town with a population of 4,983 people and 10,492 Holstein and Black Angus cattle. We are many farmers and small-business folk, some personnel from IBM down the river, a few ex-urbanites (they raise the Black Angus), and a handful of "Riverbank" aristocrats whose ancestors helped win the Revolution. A sketch of the Catskills "lording it" over the river valley graces the first page of "Rip Van Winkle." Washington Irving stood near our town when he studied that splendid view of the mountains. Our thunderstorms still strike as suddenly and are as loud as those he described.

Every June, faithful reports of college graduations appear in the local paper. According to the *Gazette*, these sons and daughters—with their newly won degrees from Cazenovia, say, or St. Bonaventure, the U.S. Coast Guard Academy, Penn State, or Harvard—bear a mysterious resemblance to each other, as in their pictures in the school yearbook. But behind the bland portraits and the standardized *Gazette* columns are real young people, and our town is a rich source of stories of their lives for any one with time to watch and listen.

Every September, for four years in a row, one of our barbers has been closing his shop in order to drive his son, Vince, to the University of Pittsburgh. "I can't figure out what studying will do for him. He's majoring in history. Three thousand dollars a year to learn about a lot of dead people. Holy Mary!" Mr. Russo, scissors in hand, makes a dangerous gesture expressing bewilderment. However, he's forbidden Vince to help pay his expenses with a campus job. It might interfere with his education! His boy's own vague motive for going to college was to qualify for a good job and get 400 miles from home. Vince was proud of the university's skyscraper, "The Tower of Learning," but he was more satisfied that he got to know students with a much greater variety of backgrounds and interests than he'd encountered here in our county. They came not only from cities but some of them from New England and even the South. He fell in with a couple of physics majors and attended their bull sessions, far into the night. One of them was a philosopher who could convince you that Galileo's law of inertia explains the relations of people along with the motion of bodies, or that Heisenberg's principle of indeterminacy can be better applied to the behavior of humans than of subatomic particles. But Vince's roommate provided an even more fundamental sort of instruction. They've lived together successfully for two years. Vince is an only child, and very orderly. The roommate comes from a large family, and isn't. "One day I found him using *my* toothbrush." They've worked out a compromise. The other fellow can live in squalor. But Vince draws a line down the middle of the room and heaves out the window anything of the roommate's he finds on the wrong side.

Contrast this experience with that of the son of our sign

painter. In my favorite recollection of Phil, he is sitting solemnly with his father in O'Leary's Bar. It is his eighteenth birthday, and he is nursing his first legal beer. His academic record in high school was poor, but he had done excellent work in art. Though a nearby college accepted him as a promising art major, he dropped out after a year and disappeared into the Armed Forces. But he came back and went on to a master's degree in art education, and when the position of art teacher in our high school opened up he received the appointment. In one of Phil's first projects, he taught the boys and girls to make kites in the ancient Chinese style. One breezy day, brilliant dragons, tigers, and carp towered over our very Occidental community.

The parents of Vince and Phil left the college choice up to the candidate and the high school counselor. Other parents are more susceptible to pressures of social and professional ambition: they may be impressed by the antiquity of those eight colleges in the Ivy League, the flair of the Little Three of the Potted Ivy League, the chic of the Seven Sisters. Seniors in our high school can be driven into trying for such schools by parents who feel anxious, if not desperate, about status.

One of our most successful businessmen considered an Ivy League college degree for his sons to be an absolute necessity. His own college studies had been cut short by the Great Depression, and to ensure theirs he sent them away to fashionable prep schools. When the oldest, Bill, heard he had missed Princeton, a scene that might have been written by John O'Hara was played in the living room: a kid brother races in with a fistful of letters from the mailbox on the road; the letter from Princeton is shakily opened. The father then gets mad at Bill. "You've let yourself down; you've let your school down; you've let *me* down." "But Dad, I've been accepted by Dickinson." "By Dickinson? By Dickinson! Good God!"

Some of our college candidates defy such family anxiety. A daughter of one of our first families had aspired to Radcliffe but was "only" accepted at Pembroke and Penn. Julia's older brother called her at home about it from a distinguished men's college—long distance. For the first time in his life he didn't call collect, they say. He begged her to go to Pembroke. Penn is just a party school, he warned. Her parents apprehensively backed him up. To spite them and her brother she chose Penn. But she now congratulates herself on the choice. One day in her senior year, Julia stopped right on Walnut Street in Philadelphia. A humble question had struck her. "Who am I that all these charming professors should be sharing their ideas with *me?*"

For Julia the main value in college was her academic work. For another of our young men its value isn't clear at all. He's a successful student, athlete, and campus factotum at the nearest Roman Catholic college. His experience there is too rich to simplify. We sat in the living room of Maynard's small house on Market Street, the quiet of the summer day accented by the ticking of several cuckoo clocks. They burst into song before I left.

Marist College is distinguished by a cylindrical dormitory, an equable group of students, and a President urgently seeking to discover the New Catholic Education. What is the New Catholic Education? You've missed the point: it's what we're hunting for. Well, then, what's most valuable to you at Marist? Maynard thought—he couldn't say for sure—maybe getting up at 6 A.M. for crew practice on the Hudson; maybe working as a campus stringer on sports for the Poughkeepsie paper; maybe a couple of professors who are really teaching him something he values. And isn't that what you go to college for? he asked triumphantly: academic learning?

Then Maynard described his best experience: a forbidden march to the town's memorial service for Martin Luther King. They'd asked the Dean to cancel classes. He refused. But even though warned not to cut anything, most of the college quietly marched uptown anyway to the Civil War monument.

There is a community college standing on the only hill that overlooks the nearby small city which is our county seat. It's a haven for large numbers of young people caught after high school between the Scylla of four years at college—a bore or an extravagance to them (or both)—and the Charybdis of going right to work—a threat or an embarrassment. When it was founded in the 1950's, most of us assumed it would grow into a regular college—bachelor's degree, football team, and all —bringing glory to our small city, which has been only a flag stop for expresses on the Penn Central. Our snobbery's died out. The faculty teach better than in many four-year colleges; they include some stimulating eccentrics but no ultras, right or left; our young people can either meet new friends or stick by old ones, and with their associate-in-arts diploma, they can grandly transfer away for a bachelor's degree or more modestly join the IBM family here. Looking down over the Hudson Valley from the campus, they breathe easily. For adjusting to the world, it's a gentler decompression chamber than a four-year college.

Eric, oldest of five (all redheads), eased the strain there. After high school and a tour as machinist's mate in the Navy, he drifted into the community college. He has no plans for a career. "But he's not the *least* bothered by that," said his mother, with a mixture of anxiety and pride. I recall Eric at the age of about ten careening around his father's fields at the wheel of a Model A Ford stripped down to the chassis. "They *all* want to come back home and *live*," she cried out in pseudo despair. "They *like* it here," she groaned. I told Eric I supposed he was studying more electronics at the college. God, no, liberal arts. "I want to find out something about the human soul. Starting with my own."

The best money earner of the younger generation hereabouts got his only formal postsecondary education at the school of the plumbers' union that serves this region. Already Joe lives like a lord, appearing frequently in the social notes of the county's largest daily. And he may well aim to fill the shoes of our town's present school-board chairman and unofficial oligarch, who is a master plumber.

Few of those in town not bound for any college don't talk about some sort of further education. As the young man at the Mobil station filled my tank and I congratulated him on the diploma he got last spring, he assured me he was taking La Salle Extension University's correspondence course in business management. "It'll prepare me to make from $15,000 to $25,000 a year."

I feel relief whenever I encounter a young man or woman hereabouts who has made a serene decision against any advanced study at all: another maverick not caught and herded off in the Great Roundup. Here are a couple of them, George and Mollie, sitting around the dining-room table one Sunday afternoon with her family, relishing a piece of Mollie's apple pie. Her father has been a competent farmer, her mother a teacher of home economics in our high school. Mollie's kid sister, bright and pert, was to go in the fall to the community college. "You've gotta have skills to get ahead." "I have skills," interrupted Mollie, and one mouthful of the apple pie proved that. She will marry George when he gets out of the service. What about him? College? Why College? He has plenty of good friends. The bank will help him start a small business. The town's going to grow a lot. Already all sorts of services are desperately needed—you've got to make an appointment for a TV repair two weeks ahead. Mollie offered me another piece of pie.

# 5 / Admissions

*"Why did you choose this college?"*
*"Why did I choose this college? Well—ah—I didn't choose it, really. It chose me."*

Once upon a time there was a girl named Carol. She lived in upstate New York. I forget just where—Skaneateles? Canandaigua? Canajoharie? I met her when she applied to Bard College. I was Director of Admissions. Now it happened that the Admissions Committee required all candidates to take the Scholastic Aptitude Test of the College Entrance Examination Board. And one day a letter came from Carol politely saying she wouldn't. I wrote a polite letter back saying she'd have to. She replied she still wouldn't, because it made admissions unfairly one-sided. I read her letter to the Committee. Who is this baggage, they protested, to tell us what's fair and not fair? *You* tell *her* that if she doesn't take the SAT, we don't act on her application.

36

Carol's mutiny took place a little over a decade ago. At just about that time a few educators who also thought college admissions unfair began to say so publicly. Today some appear ready to do more than talk. They say they will take steps to increase the flow of information about colleges to applicants and decrease the colleges' emphasis on test scores and academic marks.

The admissions process has not been symmetrical. It has been biased in favor of the colleges. They can demand a candidate's scores on national tests like those of the College Board or the American College Testing Program, or on any number of IQ or subject-matter tests. They can demand his academic record and a personal evaluation of him by teachers, counselors, administrators, relatives, employers. They can insist that these informants tell of unfavorable as well as favorable things about him. And if the college finds out later that a school has held back facts—a spell of mental illness, a conviction for a misdemeanor, an act of plagiarism—it can accuse the school of duplicity. A college can require an interview with a candidate, conducted, if it wants, like a third-degree police interrogation. It can require him to describe himself candidly and in detail. It can ask him what he thinks are his weaknesses as well as his strengths. It can ask him to state, in writing, his aims in education and life. And if he wants financial assistance, it can ask for that otherwise strictly classified secret—his father's salary.

What can this young person demand from the college? A catalogue and brochure for applicants. The catalogue does include indisputable facts, such as the college's location. It contains course offerings, though a sizable proportion are found to be postponed or discontinued. Campus rules are included, but no word on which ones are enforced—pot was smoked all last year on the second floor in one dorm, and about a dozen coeds kept cats in their rooms in another. The catalogue includes the fees, though the tuition hike for next year came just too late for this printing. It also includes the college calendar and the institution's purposes stated in generalities: "To transmit the heritage of the past for dynamic use in the present";

or "To prepare young men and women for leadership in the world of tomorrow." The brochure usually adds an account of the prettier side of college life, reinforced by photographic cheesecake.

In addition to a catalogue, an applicant can usually get an interview with an admissions officer. How much information can he expect to get from such an interview? If he asks what sorts of campus jobs are available, or what are his chances for admission, or how others from his school have done, or how many students transfer out, mature admissions officers will try to answer responsibly. But if he asks about the teaching habits of the faculty, or the success of the college's graduates, or the students' favorite preoccupations, he will get Delphic oracles.

What about the campus tour with a student guide? How valuable is this resource? Often no more valuable than one recently described in the Columbia *Spectator*. A reporter from *Spec*, pretending he was a candidate for admissions, joined a group to tour the campus. The paper printed verbatim some of the story told by his evangelistic guide—as irony.

The College Board's Commission on Tests has opened a campaign to correct this asymmetry. That word was used by the Commission's most formidable member, Professor James S. Coleman, of Johns Hopkins University's Social Relation Department. He is a sociologist with many years of involvement in the study of young people and their education. His findings have usually gone against the conventional wisdom. Though an eminent scholar, Dr. Coleman looks—and even talks—a little like a personable lightweight boxer. But he is especially formidable because he has clear-cut proposals for strengthening the candidate's hand in the admissions poker game.

For about twenty years, authors of admissions handbooks have tried ways of helping candidates judge colleges. First, somebody tried classifying them with letter grades, like those on a school report card. Many high school seniors (and their parents) snatched hungrily at these vague clues. Then the College Board inveigled a group of colleges into publishing together *The College Handbook*. It presented tables of data about an entering class of some recent year. It listed the number of freshmen who had been high school varsity captains, who were chairmen of student councils, who were children of alumni, or who had earned College Board SAT scores of over 600. This information was not as exciting or even as understandable as each institution's stark A, B, or C "rating."

Nor was much help provided by the *Handbook*'s standardized sketches of the colleges written by their admissions or public-relations staff. Their embroidery and exaggeration provoked President Fels to more satire. He made fun of the rural college's description of its easy access to the city, the women's college's assurance of the proximity of men, the large university's boast that it has the intimacy of the small college, and the conservative institution's claim to the dynamism of the experimental. Fels found a surprising number of colleges in the *Handbook* harping on their location near a river and the direction of its flow. "Columbia remains silent about the Hudson," he marveled, "although it flows both north *and* south." But this odd preoccupation of the *Handbook* writers isn't surprising, really. The space has to be filled with trivia. It is a vacuum left by omission of the campus realities of most importance to students: the social studies at one college are first-rate but other departments not; at another the main interest of typical coeds is in finding a man and keeping him attached in pseudo matrimony, if not the real thing; the faculty of a third, officially described as student-oriented, are in fact usually as remote as mandarins.

In 1959, in *The New American Guide to Colleges*, Gene Hawes made a breakthrough. Obtaining facts by an ingenious ruse, he classified the admissions standards of most colleges in the country and expressed them in bald functional terms. These range from "Highly Competitive" (Dartmouth), through "Selects from College Preparatory Candidates" (Tulane), to "Accepts All High School Graduates" (Abilene Christian). Many admissions officers, striving for an image of selectivity, had guarded their real entrance standards more jealously than coaches their teams' plays and signals. They felt threatened. But they relaxed when they found Hawes's transcontinental broadcast of their admissions standards did not jeopardize their enrollment. So they weren't especially worried when, in the 1960's, new commercial handbooks came out adding further touches of fact to the data of the Board's *Handbook* and the Hawes *Guide:* the intensity of interest of a student body in study, football, religion; the number winning national awards; the percentage who leave campus during weekends.

But none of the capsules published on or off campus suggests enough of the variety of the experience of eighteen- or nine-teen-year-olds at college. And the data by now piled up in these directories is so dense it can be interpreted easily only by those who can sift and analyze it with the skill of a detective. "What, my dear Holmes, do you make of the fact, reported in A *Comparative Guide to American Colleges,* that Columbia has a rule against throwing objects out the window?" "Ah, yes, it's the little things, Watson." Judging from the one on Columbia, *Barron's Profiles of American Colleges* do offer a digestible mixture of helpful data and comment.

Though admissions people have relaxed a little, their flow of platitudes has not subsided. But wait a minute. Suppose we could make the facts and issues all clearer to candidates. Would they be interested? Do they want that much information about colleges? Many choose one simply because it's near, or because it's far, or because they know some students there, or because it's vaguely famous. Those who do try to choose with what they think is more discrimination say they want the best college. What do they mean—"best"? The one that's the hardest to get into—irrespective of any other merit the institution may possess. "Duke rejected two out of three last year," they advise each other. "Oberlin three out of four. Wesleyan's average College Board score is now over 675. I hear Michigan's out-of-state rejection rate is getting real hairy."

Those are all reasonable rules of thumb for choosing a college. But candidates tell me they depend on them for lack of anything better. They don't like the platitudes. They would much rather have facts to help them make a more careful choice: they would appreciate knowing that at Princeton the quality of life might be quite different for a student if he came from a public rather than from a private secondary school, or that at Earlham, a small, friendly, Midwestern Quaker college, a new group of intense Eastern scholars has sharply split the campus community. I know freshmen who are stimulated rather than upset on their first arrival at a city university when a rude taxi driver dumps them in front of a building five times bigger than any in Polkville, or the dorm proctor says a freshman down the corridor just had two suitcases stolen, along with the watch he won as Goshen County Orator of the Year.

One admissions office *has* really relaxed. New York University has begun to feature in its publicity not the few trees in Washington Square or the Edith Wharton townhouses precariously surviving there or the small-scale charm of some of its Greenwich Village surroundings, but the problems of students in a large university in a large city.

The colleges have reluctantly changed their domineering ways before. They used to force all applicants to state their first-choice colleges when they took the College Board's tests. They used to require that the scores be disclosed only to admissions officers. The students, their parents, and the guidance counselors, it was feared, would misunderstand and abuse knowledge of these scores. But colleges still keep their stranglehold in other ways. Can it be broken?

Well, can it? What do you think? You've read my digest of the twenty-year struggle away from the bias in admissions. How is the struggle going now? You can tell best by following the response to the latest proposal for reform made by the College Board's Commission on Tests. The most solid part of the proposal was put in a "brief" written by James Coleman and published first in the Fall, 1969, issue of the *College Board Review*. It consists of three recommendations: first, a national standarized test of colleges, which they would be required to undergo; second, a reorganization of the College Board to represent the interests of applicants as well as of college admissions officers; third, a new emphasis in admissions on the accomplishments of candidates outside of their academic studies.

About fifteen years ago a test for colleges was developed, which might have helped admissions candidates in their planning. Called the "College Characteristics Index," it was spon-

sored by the College Board, quietly tried out in experiments
here and there, and revised to be more meaningful. A similar
test of campuses is the College and University Environment
Scale. The acronym for that title is CUES. When the CCI or
CUES is administered, a large number of students, faculty, and
administrators at one institution respond, yes or no, to several
hundred statements like these (taken from an early version of
the College Charateristics Index): "Students here spend a lot
of time at the snack bars, taverns, and in one another's rooms."
"Many committees have both faculty and student members."
"Family social and financial status may not be talked about,
but everyone knows who's who." "Students almost never see
the professors except in class." "Doing the assigned work is not
enough to win approval here." "If a student gets into trouble,
he has to find his way out."

From the comments of a large number of people on each
campus to many such statements, data emerges that can be
organized manageably under interesting headings. These would
help distinguish campuses by their tendency toward various
intellectual, social, and vocational styles and practices: Are the
faculty at Stanford more interested in teaching than the faculty
at Harvard? Are fraternities at Southern Methodist University
declining in effectiveness compared with those at Texas University? Is the proportion of students who said they were satisfied with their education (not necessarily a good sign, by the
way) larger at Denison or DePauw?

What colleges would take the test? All of them that want
test scores from students; for Coleman fortified his proposal
with this fiat:

A college won't be given test scores or other objective information
about any applicants unless it gives all applicants any comparably
hard information they want about itself.

Are college educators seriously considering this controversial
reform—yet? Are they willing to undergo systematic, objective
analysis and reveal the results?

Secondly, how about Coleman's proposal for reorganization
of the College Board? Does the Board still represent just col-

leges and school officialdom, or are applicants now represented on it? Dr. Coleman suggested adding high-school-student members, with power, to the present Board or—perhaps better—creating a division of it solely to protect applicants. Either step could counterbalance the rule of the present membership of college officials, together with principals, headmasters, and guidance counselors who collaborate like satraps with the colleges. Have you read or heard more about some such project for redistribution of authority?

What has been the general response to Coleman's third and most fundamental recommendation? What is yours? I refer to his proposal that for college-admissions decisions the nonacademic interests of candidates be counted at least as important as their academic record. Dr. Coleman was chosen champion for this cause since he had made similar paradoxes plausible before. He demonstrated once that our best public schools, the famous ones in affluent suburbs, are the least effective in college preparation. He took as his criterion not their admissions record but the later academic growth of their graduates. Since then, in a $1.5 million federal research project, he has demonstrated that the quality of the education of young blacks depends not on facilities but on attitudes of fellow students. This revelation disappointed numerous liberals and conservatives who had hoped that the black education problem could be solved by dollars.

Dr. Coleman is challenging the predominant use of academic material for the evaluation of students. He proposes that a system be designed so that a high school student's competence in coin collecting be as usable in admissions as his competence in chemistry or in getting off unusually quick punts. Consider, for example, three of this year's Columbia freshmen. One seventeen-year-old runs an investment company, which last year had sales of over a million dollars. Another has been publishing rock-music reviews regularly in a metropolitan magazine. A third has made a fine collection of spiders. Those feats demonstrate technical knowledge of finance, music, the Arachnida, as well as the skills of analysis, writing, research, and the character traits of persistence, responsibility, initiative. It's safe to assume those candidates were given as serious consideration for admission as another capable of very deceptive lateral motion in the backfield.

The accomplishments of thousands of candidates, however, less spectacular but equally promising, are missed or are not taken seriously as admissions credentials. At best, they may be discussed in an interview or described a little in an application, but usually not fully enough to reveal whether the person is a dabbler or a virtuoso. So, according to the proposal, a weather buff, an astronomy freak, or a bird watcher could ask, if he wanted, to be examined on his special knowledge. This attainment would then be presented to admissions officers along with his attainments in U.S. history, Shakespeare, or quadratic equations, and presented just as formally.

What have you perceived of the recent progress of this idea? Does the optional Student Descriptive Questionnaire, about to be administered with the Scholastic Aptitude Test, come near implementing James Coleman's proposal? Do you see ways by which it could be better done?

Possibly the response to the College Board's new challenge will be a grand swing away from all systematic evaluation and prediction, even as humane as that in the Coleman brief. Prediction and precise evaluation may be a craze. Man's passion for certainty seems directly proportional to his inability to achieve it. If he ever did, he would probably be unable to endure much of it, especially if it covered the behavior of human beings. Yet we strive constantly for accurate prediction of our behavior. How successfully? Not very, it seems.

About ten years ago admissions prediction was challenged by Joshua Fishman, a former research director of the College Board. He had examined at length the validity of high school seniors' normal credentials, mainly their marks and test scores. These are at best such poor predictors of performance in college that Dr. Fishman urged educators to stop trying to predict at all. He called for "A Moratorium on Prediction."

Since then, the moratorium has been attempted in undergraduate education at some public colleges. To admit freshmen for the fall of 1970, University of Illinois took a random sample from their applicants' pool; Federal City College in Washington, D.C., admitted them in order of application, first come, first served; and the City University of New York took any graduate of a local high school. Much of the respectable world has been shocked by New York's apparent capitulation. What will happen to the elite students if the university is geared to losers? The respectable world may not have heard the news from Alexander Astin, research director of the American Council on Education. He has found strong evidence that the value of students' education lies more in what they bring to a college than in what they get from it. An able student, Dr. Astin suggests, may learn significantly little more at Harvard than at Alderson-Broaddus or at Central Nebraska State. He wonders how long some admissions offices will go on trying only to "pick winners." He speculates that faculty may have been encouraging this cautious practice from fear of students who may need to be taught.

Fortunately or unfortunately, many private colleges may have to return soon to the virtually open admissions that was universal among them from the seventeenth century until the 1940's. In the financial crunch already threatening them all, many will have to reduce scholarship budgets sharply. We will then be retaught the once familiar truth that most willing students may be expected to carry college studies if they and their parents can pay the bill. Prediction of that qualification should be relatively easy.

In any case, watch developments carefully as the college and the candidate face each other on ever more equal terms. And imagine, finally, the feelings of Carol as she watches, too. How she must have gloated—up there in Cattaraugus—if she read in the papers this past year that Bowdoin College has given up requiring the Scholastic Aptitude Test of the College Board, as far as I know the first among leading institutions to do so. And why did Bowdoin, a bastion of Maine caution, take the lead? Could it be that those Down Easters—like Carol—have a keener sense of symmetry than the rest of us?

# 6 / Marks

*Grey grinding, I know the mind*
*That makes the great grey mill grind.*
—SAMUEL MENASHE

In a high school English class in the 1920's, Doc Strong used to make each of us recite at least once every day. He marked our recitation with a number from one to ten. I remember him calling on us, up and down the rows of desks, while our top scholar—usually a young wizard named Eddie Perkins—held the little black book and recorded the marks Doc sang out as he plowed along. "How many assassins did Macbeth send out to kill Banquo?" "Two." "Wrong. Zero. Next!" We adored Doc but hated Shakespeare.

A sophomore who works part time in my office was reading the *Odyssey* at his desk one day in late June. Summer-school course? No, this year's humanities. Why read it again? Because

you can't enjoy reading things in a course. Why not? You have
to go too fast. And they're going to mark you on it.

A couple of years ago, two of our Columbia professors gave
all their students straight A's. Their purpose was not to challenge the marking system but to help keep some young men
out of Vietnam. If a D would thrust someone toward the
battlefield, give him an A. Still, the action of these two professors made a lot of us ask each other, "Just what is the purpose of marks?"

We asked the same question at the time of the revolt at
Columbia in the spring of 1968. Classes were officially ended
for the rest of the term. Students could waive their marks and
receive a "pass." But the university rocked with argument over
the merits of the revolt. And many faculty and students continued to meet. I sat in with a U.S. history professor and one
of his classes on a lawn where police blackjacks had been
bashing heads not long before. They were discussing the difference between authority and power, with a degree of attention to the historical background of the issue rare in any classroom. Yet they were not to be marked for the extra understanding of government, education, and themselves gained
during this time. Again, some of us asked ourselves, "What
do marks record, anyway?"

American educators did not give marks to college students
until two centuries after the founding of Harvard. As far as
I can tell, our early students worked, when they did, in order
not to fall behind in their quest for salvation or in their preparation for the few colonial professions. They might also have
gotten a flogging, like the two Harvard freshmen at the first
commencement in our collegiate history. Marks were introduced at Yale in the late eighteenth century and soon dropped.
Early in the nineteenth, the faculty tried again. The habit
caught on and was soon developed into a marking system
called the "Scale of Merit." It swept through our colleges like
an epidemic. It was the system inflicted on us by Doc Strong,
an old timer who had probably learned it at Amherst College
in the 1880's.

In earlier days, for the Scale of Merit, a single fraction was used at the end of the year to express the student's performance in all subjects: the bottom figure showed what his total would have been if he had answered every daily question perfectly, the top figure the total he did achieve. In 1862, at Bard College, for instance, Philip Kimber's score for his junior year was this: 2,988 over 3,221; Andrew Schoonover's was 1,528 over 3,177. Schoonover's low score may also reflect nonacademic backsliding, for the faculty gave students demerits for misconduct and then subtracted these from the numerator of those fractions. Andrew may have been caught too many times reading novels, playing cards, or using the ten-pin alley at forbidden hours.

American higher education was at its worst during that time. A Harvard alumnus complained that if imaginative men had labored to design something most likely to turn young people away from learning, they would have come up with our mid-nineteenth-century college programs. The crowning touch to their masterpiece would have been the Scale of Merit.

A revolt against it began soon after the Civil War. One of the leading insurgents was Frederick Augustus Porter Barnard, President of Columbia University. He confronted an adamant faculty. They insisted that unless marked constantly and meticulously, college students would do no work. Barnard asked them why students had worked in the days before marks were introduced. He recalled that the only evaluation of his own Class of 1828 at Yale had been a ranking of them all in their junior year, arrived at by a vote among themselves.

Reformers have been unable to abolish the Scale of Merit completely. They did get rid of the daily recitation and the demerits. But midterm and final marks continue to punctuate, if not define, the academic procedure. That big yearly fraction has been given up, too. Nevertheless, the Registrar today takes a jumble of course marks earned over four years and converts it into a student's average—sometimes to three decimal places.

What does a 3.92 average record? Much too often it records mainly skill at getting a 3.92 average.

I once taught in an elementary school where the younger pupils weren't given marks at all. Third graders would read, write, and talk eagerly about their studies with no motive but Homeric curiosity. When we began giving marks to our fourth graders, they reacted like the Indians to whiskey—they were hooked. They began to work for the marks.

I saw the same thing happen to college students when I was working at Bard College in the early 1950's. Few professors gave examinations to their students, and none gave marks. A lot of hard and imaginative academic work was done. But instead of marking it, the faculty evaluated it on what were called "Criteria Sheets," one for each student in each course, under headings like "Amount of work done," "Originality," "Class discussion," "Use of resourses," "Written work," and "Comments." A history professor wrote this comment about Sophomore Herbert Rondell: "Disorganized term paper on effects of Civil War but interesting idea about its impact on William Faulkner. Read widely beyond recommended list. Not overlogical but thoughtful, even poetic—maybe should switch major to literature." The students read these sheets eagerly. Then, during the Korean War, the Selective Service System required colleges to rank all male students. To do this more easily, the Bard faculty began to use marks. I soon noticed that Herb talked less about the Civil War and more about the marks he hoped he'd get.

The intemperate response of students to marks probably vitiates their effect more than anything else. And this is not a recent vice among students. The only form of evaluation I have found in the record of medieval universities—except for the diploma—is a ranking of his students by each professor when he presented their names to the chancellor as successful candidates for graduation. One gathers that the order may have sometimes been determined by social standing or even by mere hanky-panky. But the students obviously took it too seriously, anyway, since a professor was advised to make up his list and turn it in quickly to escape pestering by the early equivalent of the grade hound—*ne importunis sollicitetur.*

What about the pedagogical value of marks? One of the most serious technical objections to them is their unreliability. Careful experiments have shown that experienced instructors will often mark the same piece of student work very differently, and the judgment of one instructor, marking it more than once, may seesaw crazily.

Alfred North Whitehead, Harvard's great philosopher of the early twentieth century, said he preferred B students. He concluded that a student industriously earning A's had little energy left over for creative thought. Whitehead also perceived the typical A student as a conformist, scouting out the academic fashion, psyching the professors, and then responding with finesse. In fact, that describes the performance of all too many B and C students, too—they simply don't work so hard at it.

If marks are questionable, then, as a record of performance, how valuable are they as a stimulus to effort?

For several decades, students in some colleges have been doing good work without the influence of any marks. At Reed and Bennington they don't see their marks at least until graduation—when not many of them care any more. Yet Reed and Bennington alumni have been judged as well educated as those from any of our campuses. Indeed, at one time—allowing for its size—Reed was said to be producing a larger number of productive scientists than any college in the nation. At Goddard and Sarah Lawrence colleges no marking has ever been done, even clandestine. Have their graduates suffered? The Brown University faculty, like a number of other faculties, have been recently offering all students the "pass-fail" option in several courses to encourage them to range into remote and therefore more difficult subjects. Convinced by the students' response to that experiment, Brown has just given up marks entirely. The experience of these several institutions strongly suggests that young people do not need marks as an incentive to learn.

What about another widely held view of marks: that they predict future effectiveness? Late last century, American college students thought they did. High academic standing now, they told each other, means occupational mediocrity later; it's safer to get C's; employers don't want to hire grinds; worse yet, reading and study weaken character. So vast numbers of collegians scrupulously avoided A's and B's. Not long before

World War One, President Lowell of Harvard complained that respect for intellect among American students, including his own, had fallen to its lowest point in civilized history. Finally, Dr. Lowell dug into the records of his Registrar and Alumni offices. He was able to publish data suggesting that scholastically high-ranking graduates often enough do achieve worldly success later.

Unfortunately, the nation has overreacted to Lowell's idea. Today a majority of our students have turned their grandfathers' superstition upside down. They fear mediocrity if they do *not* earn high marks. They've been sold at home, school, and college on the supreme importance of amassing blue-ribbon academic credentials for further education or for a career. And the worst of it is that bucking for good marks to ensure a successful career probably interferes more with the liberal education of the modern young puritans who now crowd our campuses than evading good marks did to our early-twentieth-century collegiate hedonists. So far, no realists of the stature of Lowell have tried seriously to point that out.

A very small amount of evidence does suggest that from academic marks later effectiveness can be projected. The management at American Telephone and Telegraph say they hire only college graduates with good academic marks—top third or so. They insist that according to the company's records the higher the marks, the better the performance at A T & T—in salary. They swashbuckle around a little over all this. Some of us suspect it may be an ingenuous statistical self-deception. The only other supposedly objective recent evidence I've seen that good marks are correlated with later success came from Brown University. It seems the incomes of the A students in a class that graduated a decade or two ago were compared with those of its C students. The A's reported average incomes somewhat higher than those of the C's.

Most of the careful studies I've seen or read about reveal no such predictive power in marks. According to one, the higher-ranking medical student excels technically in his practice for a few years but then is overtaken by his classmates. Otherwise, the systematic modern evidence indicates that a college student's future cannot be predicted from his academic marks.

The most ruthless use of marks today is in the admissions procedures of elite law schools. Not that marks predict future academic performance there better than elsewhere. Nor do they predict future effectiveness in the law. A number of law school admissions officials have privately confessed discomfort bordering on disillusionment over their admissions procedure. "We know it's unfair. But with all those applicants, what else can we do?" A couple of years ago the Dean of Admissions of one eminent school wrote a letter to a large number of college prelaw advisers asking them to suggest improvements. Until someone succeeds, marks, supported by scores on the Law School Admission Test, will simplify the task of selection from an army of candidates, a high percentage of whom are well qualified. So even though admitting those with the highest marks doesn't select better law students, let alone better lawyers, it seems logical and therefore good legal style.

If marks are deceptive as a record of performance, unnecessary as an incentive, and useless as a predictor, what good are they? In a word, they're a convenience. For educators and employers do need to choose among people. Even if their method of choice doesn't stand careful inspection, they can all ignore that distraction and go right on choosing with it—as long as enough of the rest of us accept it and as long as it's convenient for everyone.

We may have developed our marking system simply out of our American need to be counting, ranking, and rating everything. This habit may have come from our insecurity. As a new, fluid society, we invent new structures to shape life. Numbers provide a useful framework. We describe a halfback by his rushing yardage, a painting by its price, a book by its place on the best-seller lists, and an applicant for some education or job opportunity by his academic average. But isn't the development of less ramshackle structures one of the benefits education should confer?

This past spring term I taught the same course, Advanced Career Development, in two graduate schools of education,

Bank Street's and Fordham's. The experience, otherwise de-
lightful and exciting, went sour at the end when I had to mark
the students. One of the finest features of it, the sharp difference between the two groups, then became a headache: Bank
Street's Protestant or Jewish students, who teach or counsel in
elementary or high school; Fordham's Roman Catholics, two of
them priests and six sisters, including a number attached to
colleges. Progressive Bank Street questioning, even contentious;
pious Fordham responsive but quiet and deferent. So, in trying
to judge them all against the same criterion, I was comparing
apples and oranges. Worse still, Bank Street offers only three
passing marks: A, B, and C; while Fordham offers everything
from A+ to C—. Some who got Bank Street's C would have
gotten Fordham's B.

And how mark Miss Judith Applebaum, who could not do
enough of the career interviewing required because her part of
the city was too dangerous? How count my poor communication with Mr. Patrick Casey, who wrote a beautiful, scholarly,
original term paper on competence in careers, but which was
unrelated to the people he'd interviewed? And how weigh the
fine pipe and tobacco pouch presented to me by Mr. Carlos
Lopez?

Oh, well. If asked to teach again at either school, I may do
what a friend of mine did last year. He's a very successful advertising account executive who left Madison Avenue to teach
writing to college undergraduates. His first term he asked his
students to mark themselves. He was amazed at their fairness.
In his judgement, only one out of the two dozen overrated his
work, and only two or three underrated theirs. Or maybe I'll
let them choose: the less secure souls, who crave to be marked,
may be granted that favor, and bolder ones, who want a
greater challenge, may mark themselves. The most earnest may
evaluate their work in the course by its effect upon their life
and thought.

# 7 / Faculty

*"Oh, Callias," Socrates asked his friend. "You and your sons, have you found a teacher for them? Someone who understands virtue—virtue in politics, virtue in life, virtue in itself? You must have been looking."*

*"Yes, I have found one."*

*"Splendid, who is he? And where does he come from?"*

*"His name is Evenus, and he comes from Paros. They say he's quite a teacher. And his fee, by the way, is only five minae."*

*"Generous man," Socrates sighed, "to know so much and charge so little. If I were that wise, I'd make a fortune. But here I am an old ignoramus who has to teach for nothing."*

The lightning of student protest has hardly begun to flicker around the teaching faculty. Even the blacks, though moved by academic grievances, have usually taken administrators for their immediate target. Do protesters single out the Dean because they know they can find him in? More probably because they see him as a wielder of power. That threatens many young people. They see faculty as working with ideas. That disarms them. So, reports of the National Student Association show very little campus protest aimed directly at academic abuses. The orators of the student revolution have condemned the curriculum. All but the blacks, however, have passed on quickly to other outrages: the war, the Pentagon and big-business fascism, university exploitation of neighborhood poor, autocracy on campus. By comparison, academic reform appears to be a complex and gray issue. And it means tackling that enigma, the faculty.

The enigma comes out of the confusion caused by four paradoxes. First, the academic faculty seem weak in the campus power structure, but in fact they are strong. Second, they are archindividualists who form a well-knit brotherhood. Third, they serve the society, yet are models of detachment. Fourth, they are expected to be at once devoted teachers and aggressive scholars.

Paradox Number One: the weakness of strength. Professors are occupationally descended from the slaves who were the scholars and teachers of ancient Rome and from the medieval priests who created the modern university. Many have inherited an attitude of detachment from the world, perhaps a fear of it. America's typical professor for two and a half centuries was a Protestant parson who could not get or hold a pulpit. His early image was impractical, that of a dreamer. Today professors do pursue scientific truth. This is a gentler occupation than the pursuit of power, status, or money. They are also trying to pass along the heritage, a quieter occupation than adding to it. And according to two careful studies of professors' hours spent at teaching, advising, preparation, committees, and endless scholarly research, a large proportion put in hours like those of the better-publicized doctor or top business executive. Much of their long summer vacation goes into intensive, urgent study. They do much of this for love. And that last notion has helped the society rationalize paying professors less than most other professionals. Don't their psychic rewards make up the balance?

But beginning in the middle of the last century, when serious scholars multiplied on our campuses, the title of professor also acquired the connotation of great expertise. A balloonist, a mind reader, or a pianist in a brothel could use it. Industry finally added glamour to this image by turning to university faculties for ideas and technical help. Late last century, state governments, too, most notably Wisconsin's, began to seek professors as consultants not only in agriculture but in business and even in politics. Then Woodrow Wilson's presidency and

Franklin D. Roosevelt's Brain Trust lent the professorial image national prestige. But after young Professor James Bryant Conant developed poison gas during the First World War, the image began to take on the look of a Frankenstein creating the monster that will destroy him—and the rest of us. And the look has been given an extrasinister, Dr. Strangelove cast by unsympathetic accounts of Professor Henry Kissinger in the White House brainwashing President Nixon. Nevertheless, sociologists find that the American people, when questioned about the status of occupations, put college professors near the top, close to Congressmen, diplomats, and mayors of large cities.

Not only has their social prestige and political power increased, so has their influence in the running of our colleges and universities. Christopher Jencks and David Riesman, in their book, *The Academic Revolution*, describe the revolution as a takeover of power, not by students but by faculty.

Faculty power was negligible in the early days of American colleges and universities. From the seventeenth century to the end of the nineteenth, American higher education was dominated by trustees and especially by presidents. Before the Civil War, trustees often conducted oral final examinations of students and took a direct hand in their discipline. At the same time, presidents bullied their faculties, which were small and professionally unorganized.

After the Civil War, however, when professors adopted the model of the German scholar, their power began to grow. By the end of the century, it was embodied in a degree system so deadly that William James could nickname it "the Ph.D. Octopus." By 1915, professorial power was institutionalized in the American Association of University Professors, which since then has remained wholly preoccupied with improving academic salaries and censuring brash administrators for threatening "academic freedom" and tenure rights. By now, college and university faculty have become an international brotherhood of specialists, with iron control over the educational process. Their power is especially important to students: the degrees they award are symbols of the key that opens the door into the meritocracy.

So, like a coin, their image has something different on each side. On one side is the absent-minded professor. As a boy in the 1920's, I used to hear many stories about him. Coming home on a rainy day, he kisses his umbrella and stands his wife in the sink. On the other side is a person of high competence. When Lefty Grove laid down one of his perfect bunts, someone in the stands behind me commented "He's like a professor."

During the campus troubles of the last few years, I've heard older faculty dwell on the weakness of the university as an institution in society. "It's so fragile. It's as vulnerable as a mollusk without a shell." Those are the words of a distinguished historian in conversation after a fine dinner of the Faculty Club. They do not ring true. More probably, faculty are anxious because deep down they know *they* must change the university. It isn't weak. It's awkward. It's overdeveloped, like a brontosaurus. His bulk was his downfall. Similarly, the strength of our faculty may be their weakness. They are musclebound.

Paradox Number Two: individuality vs. solidarity. Back in the early 1800's, the finest days of the University of Berlin, the great linguistic pioneer Wilhelm von Humboldt was made the Rector. In that position he saw for the first time how individualistic his fellow faculty were. He wrote his wife a letter comparing them to "a troupe of second-rate actors." He said he was appalled at their preoccupation with advantages, not only for their own department over others but for themselves over their departmental colleagues. The American university imported much of its philosophy and practice from the German, including this jealous habit. A mathematician, pleasant, competent, and undistinguished, is hired by a distinguished university and promptly appointed chairman of his department. His new colleagues were engaged in an internal brawl and would have cut any one of their own number into pieces.

The most compelling motive of young people for entering the academic profession is the desire for independence. In the college classroom their teaching will be unsupervised. There will be almost no fetters on their self-expression, and according to their students, the more personality they put into their teaching the better, provided they hold to good scholarly standards.

And their colleagues and superiors will tolerate a surprising amount if the eccentricity isn't associated with some cause too heady for the time and circumstances. A Columbia instructor may have gone too far when he rolled a motorcycle into his class on Utopias and Freedom and revved her up. Was it for this stunt that his reappointment failed to come through? Perhaps his department perceived other limitations in him.

College faculty must also venture solo into their scholarly research. Whether or not this turns out to be creative, they do it independently. They search for and follow up ideas among their books and papers the way a trapper follows his lines. A Haverford alumnus wrote in his college memoirs of a lonely Christmas Eve on campus. He recalled his comfort at the sight of a light burning on after midnight in a professor's study. Does the path of epsilon rays through a vacuum accord better with the wave or with the corpuscular theory? In what way was human sacrifice among pre-Columbian Indians compatible with the spirit of their welfare state? On what journey to what worlds had that solitary scholar embarked?

Teaching and scholarship are a very independent trip—psychedelic but nonpharmaceutical. On the other hand, faculty are highly organized as a group. About credentials they are strict. They measure the strength of an institution by the percentage of Ph.D.'s among its faculty. They measure the status of a colleague by the eminence of the university that granted his most advanced degree. They measure his promise by the books and articles he has published, even though, as Professors Caplow and McGee show in their study, *The Academic Marketplace*, most of the research literature is not read by anybody. One European observer suggested it might best be evaluated by weight.

In their hierarchy, faculty rank themselves as strictly as the Armed Forces. The titles are nearly as numerous: preceptor, teaching assistant, lecturer, adjunct, assistant, associate, full professor, and finally the university professor, the five-star general, who is over and above all departments and disciplines. The hierarchy is most visible at commencement, when faculty march in scrupulous order. The bachelors, masters, and doctors are recognized by the length of the sleeves of their gowns, their college or university origin by the colors or materials of their hoods—the solid luminous crimson of Harvard, the rabbit-fur trimmings of Oxford. The academic procession sways down the aisle as bright as a new tapestry, as structured as an Army column.

In their system of control the faculty more and more emulate the medieval guild, from which they are occupationally descended. They maintain the guild tradition better than any other profession today. A few years ago, David B. Truman, former Dean of Columbia College, now President of Mount Holyoke, declared that a professor in any of our elite colleges and universities is no longer attached—in the emotional sense of the word—to the campus where he holds a position; rather, he is attached to his scholarly discipline—biology, political science, linguistics. But this attachment is so firm that he can migrate from campus to campus with the ease of a nomad.

This unusual combination of individualism and conformity is not unique to the academic profession. Sociologist Seymour Lipset found other occupational groups that strikingly resembled professors, namely, miners, lumbermen, and fishermen. Their kind of work tends to cut them off from the rest of the world as it exposes them closely and often to each other. In part unusually individualistic, in part unusually cohesive, they will pull together well if pitted against an important opponent. Sometimes they do this with especially cavalier disregard even for their own interests. Afternoon papers early in the Second World War carried these headlines:

MARINES BADLY MAULED ON GUADALCANAL

WEST COAST FEARS INVASION

MINE WORKERS STRIKE

Professors will usually close ranks most readily against administrators. Two years ago I listened for ten or fifteen hours to testimony by several dozen people, including many faculty, before a commission investigating the causes of student unrest at Columbia. I did not hear one of them blame anyone for it but the administrators and trustees. They came down especially hard on the President. This was no great surprise to me. A couple of years earlier, a Cornell professor described to me his colleagues' similar reaction after the first revolt at Berkeley. News had reached Ithaca of the students' manifesto putting the blame for the revolt on the Berkeley administration. The assembled Cornell faculty resolved to telegraph to California an endorsement of the manifesto. They had not read it, but when someone moved that the resolution be held up until they could, he was briskly overruled. It was enough to know from the news media that the Berkeley students were condemning the university's administrative arm.

Observers have speculated that the professional schizophrenia of the college professor—"Am I an independent or a cog in a wheel?"—is aggravated by the late-adolescent identity crisis of many of his students. Their affliction may be contagious. He does his own thing yet conforms rigidly. He is absorbed in some solitary quest, yet his profession is as tightly organized as the electrical workers'. This extreme range of style keeps college professors, as an occupational group, anxious and defensive. It keeps their students puzzled about them.

Paradox Number Three: public service vs. value-free inquiry. The state charters a college or university for the primary purpose of developing its young people into good citizens. Most of these attend it as a means to a good job. Many of the faculty in our leading institutions disregard both these ends. They use the institution as a private facility for their own exploration of man and the universe. They commandeer it for their own purposes the way a cuckoo takes over another bird's nest.

The academic program they offer students in general is a fallout from their own individual scholarship. Faculty assume that it will provide liberal education of civic and vocational value. They assume that currently fashionable topics—the Gestalt in psychology, continental drift in geology, the hero in European literature—if dispassionately discussed with a roomful of young men and women, will broaden and elevate them. The best of the faculty have been broadened and elevated by the tough thinking they did to develop these themes. Why shouldn't their students be, too, by exposure to them in lectures, reading, term papers, and preparation for exams? Scholars assume that a mysterious educational benefit can be derived from any contact with the specialized research now in fashion, ever more minute and pedantic.

In this assumption our faculty follow the great German scholars of the last century. They worshiped abstract ideas and attributed to them magical power. One of Germany's responses to being trampled over by an earthly emperor, Napoleon, had been to build a holy empire of the mind. Its statesmen were professors, and its religion was research. Its security lay in its detachment from the life of ordinary men. If the new Prussian military machine should fail, another invader could violate the German land and people but not that intellectual commonwealth ruled by German scholars—*Wissenschaft*, "the realm of ideas."

Unfortunately, in Germany this movement became a mystique, and professors its high priests. They were rightly regarded with considerable awe by the German people for their mental labor and learning. But this tribute went to their heads. They became proud; they cut themselves off from the business and politics of their nation and from its young people; they not only felt scorn for men of action, they expressed it openly, publicly. The combination of complacency and prestige led to the greatest disaster in the history of higher education—the sudden and unconditional surrender of Germany's universities to Hitler.

But *Wissenschaft* had inspired the ambitious young American scholars who trooped to Germany for their Ph.D.'s in the nineteenth century. They thundered with their feet as a Mommsen or a Ranke entered the lecture hall; they hung on his words in a doctoral seminar, where he taught them to analyze poetry with scrupulous objectivity and relentless method. They brought this gospel back and manfully struggled to introduce it among the Calvinist faculty and rowdy students at Denison or Dartmouth.

In this country, *Wissenschaft* has been thwarted by our old Anglo-Saxon mistrust of ideas. We sense in our bones that ideas divide, while feelings unite men. Also, it has been the tradition to have our colleges and universities supervised not by a bureaucratic government ministry, as remote as the professors, but by a reasonably decent hodgepodge of lay trustees who could respond to the leadership of a good president. Furthermore, the students have created a lively collegiate extra-curriculum that operates as a buffer protecting them from our faculty's attempt to dehumanize and Teutonize the academic system. Our faculty have even failed to block the Student Personnel Movement, in which I serve. It is now possible to earn a doctor's degree in preparation for a career as a counselor, resident-hall director, financial-aid or placement officer. This is our highly organized but still rather ineffectual effort to see to it that students are treated like human beings.

Even our most imperious faculty, because they were American, could not match the German presumption. But a few years ago many did try to, when some leading academicians made the prophecy that the university would soon become the center of our society. Word of this bravura provoked amusement in business and other professions. In students it may have helped provoke the campus riots of recent years.

On one side of the paradox, then, we see human beings on college faculties, like the philosophy professor I watched at Penn State tossing a football with a student in the corridor, or the eminent Harvard historian who never missed a varsity athletic event. On the other side of the paradox we see American faculty following Karl Mannheim, who, even after his nation's academic tragedy, promoted the concept of *Freischwebende Intelligenz*—"free-floating intelligence." This concept lies behind our faculty's inclination to present their subjects purified of utility or meaning: "Why did my sociology professor only mention morality in his last lecture?" "Why in all my courses for a major in astronomy did no professor relate it to religion?"

The irony is classic: the American academic establishment offers transcendental magic; its students passionately desire earthly knowledge.

Paradox Number Four: teaching vs. scholarship. A young instructor at Harvard in 1856, with dormitory duty, ended a letter to a friend as follows:

By Jove, there is a confounded noise up in Harrod's room this moment; this Parietal business is a nuisance, disagreeable to shirk and disagreeable to do. Getting worse and worse upstairs, singing now though it is after 11 P.M. I rather think I had better give my attention to this subject at once, so Good-bye.

Yours,<br>Charles W. Eliot

Faculty in our colonial and early national colleges concentrated on their students. But a large proportion of the concentration was on discipline. Eliot said he saw a dilemma there. How could he teach them well in the classroom if he was policing them outside? Solving problems such as that one, Eliot was to become the greatest college president in our history.

Now the terms have changed. Much of the faculty's time and energy goes into scholarship. The dilemma today is that you can't teach your students well if you are too devoted to scholarship.

The faculty began to let up on students after the Civil War. Or the students pulled away from the faculty. Either way, each party had plenty else to do—the students their newly developed campus activities, the faculty their newly imported scholarship. Each pursued his separate life like a religion. Walter Camp, the great Yale coach, had once intended to be a clergyman and indeed regarded football as a spiritual force. His alumni went forth as coaches and carried the gospel to other colleges all over the country. The faculty of our leading institutions similarly threw themselves with religious zeal into scientific study of everything from art to zoology. Academically the two sides found a compromise: the faculty substituted their new subject matter for the tired, traditional college studies but did not require the young people to work hard over it; the students gave up their hooliganism.

The two parties went their separate ways and enjoyed the truce for about seventy-five years. But early in the 1960's, one of the most representative bodies of academics, the Association for Higher Education, rediscovered students. In their annual bulletin the officers confessed that during the history of the Association's annual conferences, the item of students could not be found among the topics of discussion. They had been concentrating on such weightier topics as subject matter, academic freedom, and the future of the university.

The discovery was a great embarrassment. Faculty didn't know what to do about students. Most paid no attention. Their momentum has carried them straight on in their specialized research. Late in 1970, the American Council of Learned Societies, representing over thirty academic disciplines, published an article by a distinguished historian, William J. Bouwsma, of Berkeley and Harvard, with a confession: generally, American scholars do not know or care about education.

But in some a passion for both teaching and scholarship combine, as in Professor Henry F. Graff of Columbia. You may have read in *The New York Times Magazine* his interviews with President Johnson. He turns out good books. He serves on important university committees. And he teaches his classes with gusto. A student's recollection of one went something like this:

"We'd been told Graff is a Theodore Roosevelt freak. So we were sad there were only a few minutes left when he got to the Spanish War.

"Teddy rushed up San Juan Hill, he said, with a dozen pairs of spectacles tucked and pinned all over him. If some *caballero* knocked one off, he could whip out another and still see the whole show. He hated to miss anything. He'd always dreaded not having his bird glasses along if a prothonotary warbler or a Louisiana water thrush or a pileated woodpecker flew near.

"Also, T.R. was an anxious man underneath, Graff told us. He had a number of psychosomatic symptoms. He used to say that many of the people who've accomplished a lot didn't feel well much of the time.

"In Teddy Roosevelt, according to Graff, it's hard to disentangle the scientist, the public servant, and the neurotic. To live with himself, he had to do big things. He had to be a Giant Killer. And you shouldn't tackle a giant—Tammany Hall, the Reading Railroad, or the Spanish Empire—if you've dropped your only pair of spectacles."

Perhaps higher education is not really at its worst but at its best when taut with the tensions between the weakness and the strength of the academic man, between his individualism and his professional loyalties, between the practical uses his work is put to and the detachment he attributes to it, between the demands of teaching and study. The paradoxes of the professor's lot may present an enigma, confusing to others and nerve-racking to himself. But they may also be recognized, understood, and used to good advantage by him if he possesses energy, gusto, and a well-developed sense of tragicomedy.

The tension was well expressed last year by a retired professor at the University of California at Davis, James F. Wilson, M.A., LL.D. He strung a wire between two poles, took off his trousers, hung them over it, tossed a little kerosene on them, and struck a match. With his silver hair, steel-rimmed spectacles, and tweed jacket, the agriculture professor was photographed by United Press International watching the flames.

"This is how I express my revulsion," he told the crowd come to watch. "Revulsion over the war in Southeast Asia. Revulsion over the young idiots trying to rule and ruin our campuses."

# 8 / Freedom

*"A popgun is a popgun, though the ancient and honorable of the earth affirm it to be the crack of doom."*

*"Society everywhere is in conspiracy against the manhood of every one of its members."*

*"Be your Giant Self."*

Williams College had refused Ralph Waldo Emerson a hall on campus, so the students had hired one downtown and were listening to him for the third straight day.

George Bernard Shaw said only worthless people seek freedom and happiness, and their punishment is that they get both, only to find they have no use for the freedom and no capacity for the happiness. College helps young people grapple with the mystery Shaw was referring to. At first they feel free—like a small-town freshman at Columbia who had kept none of his appointments for the first three weeks of college. When the Dean's Office caught up with him, they found Lester had spent all day every day riding the city's subway system. "Want to get to King's Highway, Brooklyn? Okay. Take the IRT local to Fifty-Ninth Street; go downstairs and catch the D train east; get off at Seventh Avenue, and go downstairs again for an E train south to Thirty-Fourth Street; take the F train south. . . ."

On opening day, a student who attends a residential college permits his parents to help him take things from the car, meet some academic officials at the Dean's reception, and drink a glass of sweet pink punch. Then they drive away, leaving him— free. After that he begins a period of misery lasting anywhere from his freshman year until the start of his junior year. It takes him that long to accept his exchange from slavery to home and high school for the much more ruthless slavery to himself. One of our dormitory counselors says a number of freshmen go without clean laundry for a while because they don't know how to use the washing machines in the basement and are afraid to ask anybody for help. I wonder, by the way, who teaches Haverford College students how to iron? I looked into a room in the basement of Founders' Hall; there, at several boards, young men plied their steam irons, from time to time glancing at a book propped open at one end of their board.

Ask headmasters, principals, and guidance counselors how their new alumni feel when they come back to school during the Christmas vacation of their freshman year at college. A large majority confide or proclaim that higher education is a fraud and a bore, or that they went to the wrong college and they'd never go back if they dared not to. A good many do transfer or quit by the end of that year, if not first term. If they transfer, they often find that their next college choice is the right one—or a much better one. But they're probably only getting used to the feeling of the slavery of freedom.

Even at ultraconservative colleges most young people have to make more decisions than at home about alcohol, clothes, drugs, food, friends, fun, sex, and sleep. The nation boasts some very authoritarian colleges. At Bob Jones University, in South Carolina, women recently were not allowed to go into nearby Spartanburg, I'm told, unless in threes. At Atlantic Union, in Massachusetts, men had to be in by midnight, women by ten. But such authority is light compared with that which a college student must impose on himself, on any campus, if he wishes any sense of what is traditionally called happiness. "Happy here, Suzie?" I asked a Bard College sophomore, then waiting on table in the faculty dining room. "Happy? Ho, ho," she retorted sarcastically, as she hoisted her tray. "But I'll tell you what I am—I'm efficient. I now know how to study. Or at least I'm learning how," she added quickly as one of her professors at the table glared theatrically at her.

Probably the same sort of puritanical satisfaction in the stern use of freedom was expressed to me by Katherine, daughter of a Southern Air Force general, wife of a student in our Graduate School of Business, pretty as a camellia. She came to see me for advice about getting a job as a secretary. She'd transferred from a four-year women's college, which she couldn't stand, into Northern Virginia Community College. There she worked terribly hard for the first time in her life. Why all the work? Well, her father had deplored her move from a fashionable residential college to an unfashionable commuters' college. She'd show *him*. In the end she also got into mathematics. That's not regarded as a ladylike study down South, she says. "But I found it was my thing." Then why not a job using that? Here the puritanism dropped away. Katherine doesn't want a career, as she put it, but a man, a lot of children, and a house, if possible one with a neoclassical portico. Still, her college experience gave her other choices. "That's freedom," she said.

At the Greyhound Bus Terminal in Boston last summer the baggage loader's T-shirt read "Miami-Dade." I asked him to tell me about it. He told another story of freedom through struggle. He said he went to college because everybody he knew was going, and he understood Miami-Dade has good drama. It does. The drama students work harder than anyone down there except the athletes. Why so? "Because we're more on our own." Enjoy college? Hell, no, he can't wait to travel around the world writing magazine articles about it. Who helped him make that decision? I hoped he might be in touch with my colleague, the career adviser. But nobody had helped him. He decided it while lugging baggage at the bus terminal.

A writer for *Fortune* magazine asked if he could talk with a group of our seniors about their plans and goals. He wanted to test his guess that young people today aren't thinking as far ahead about their careers as he believes students used to. Their responses surprised him. Their foresight seemed as earnest as any previous generation's. The difference lay in what they're looking for—more freedom. They perceive their parents and older friends locked into a series of moves in a game, perhaps winning ones. But what price victory?

A striking proportion of college seniors say their most satisfying experience during all their years of formal education was travel during a vacation. During term time they still feel like pawns in the great bourgeois chess game. They more or less dutifully amass credits and good marks and otherwise play their part in a gambit that will contribute to some later checkmate. But since it seems like somebody else's game, no harm in turning your back on it now and then.

A freshman from an upper-class Chicago suburb told me how he did that. During Christmas vacation of his senior year of high school he persuaded the old man to let him—for the first time—take the Jaguar away somewhere, leaving the family to struggle along in the Impala. With a friend he drove south—just south. They simply followed their impulses—whoever was driving deciding where to turn. Once, they jumped out and hopped a freight train for a mile or two. "You'd been reading William Saroyan?"

Students may choose from several other varieties of trips: it may be drugs or campus protest; or it may be a motorcycle on which they disappear into a huge helmet and defy the citizenry with the roar of a 600-cc motor and the risk of sudden death; or they may choose to travel in the "realms of gold," as Keats described this sort of trip in his sonnet. In college today this could also mean travel into the realms of symbolic logic, medieval manorial economics, Gestalt psychology, rococo's evolution into neoclassicism, mass communication, high-energy particles, or high African civilizations before AD 1500.

Several students have told me of an especially enjoyable sort of academic trip. They pass through college cutting a very large proportion of their classes. Those who do this can often earn good academic standing, like the many who got by in an earlier, easier academic time. A Columbia senior in sociology reports one close shave in which he was rescued by an imaginative professor. Avoiding all books on the course list, he read widely in the field. But after a look at the final exam, he gave up and turned in his blue book untouched. He went the next day to the professor to apologize. Wanting to know what this young man had gotten from his own reading, the prof conversed with him for three hours and gave him a straight A.

In their need to move, as in many other traits, students today resemble the wandering scholars of the Middle Ages. Then, as now, students transferred in large numbers from university to university, like the 350,000 American students who will do that this year. Many of them also toted a stringed instrument, and they, too, were creating a student culture with its own dress, language, and songs. Their words and music, recorded in Carl Orff's *Carmina Burana*, closely resemble today's rock music. They had their own saint, as ours have Dylan. They used even more force to support their demand for better education, and they were resented even more by the townspeople, who murdered several hundred of them. One difference was that after the bloodshed, the authorities sternly took the side of the students.

The consequences of freedom are always challenging, often difficult, and sometimes dire. Young people don't need wiseacres like you and me to point out that moral. They get it themselves, whether after a demonstration, a march, a commune, or an escape to Canada. The cost may be an overheated engine getting there, sharp anxiety, forfeiture of credentials—or of citizenship. It may be a dozen stitches on the scalp. That the educational value is great was pointed out to me by a dropout from another Ivy League college whom I met on the first day of the Columbia troubles in the spring of 1968. He'd heard something was up here and made it through one of the campus gates with a friend's identification card. Too bad, I said, taking in the milling crowd, the various colored rebel arm bands, the red flag on one of the university buildings, and the two or three police commanders already studying the terrain. On the contrary, he argued; this is the first time in fifteen years of formal education that students have been able to think of all that applesauce they've been served and ask themselves, Do I want it? They came to college for more education, and this is it, man.

The educational value of that event, together with the tribulations that accompany growth and freedom, is clear in the experience of Stanley Psczsylkowski, who came to Columbia from Sherman's Creek, in western Pennsylvania. He had distinguished himself in high school, especially as football captain, and had been committed by his high school faculty and most of his family and friends to attend Shippensburg or another state teachers college or, at worst, Penn State. They liked Stan the way he was.

Well, even after two years at Columbia, Stan insists he was still pure Sherman's Creek. Then, in the spring of his sophomore year came the Bust. Stan saw five buildings barricaded, students fighting students, students jeering at faculty, police knocking both unconscious, and the university brought to a halt. Like thousands of young people in scores of colleges, these events made him begin to think for the first time in his life. He thought about education, he thought about government, he thought about himself. Everything he read, heard, did, took on more meaning.

"Ever read Thomas Wolfe's book *You Can't Go Home Again?*" Stan asked. The length of his hair, hardly noticeable on Manhattan's Upper West Side, looked too long back on Elm Street. Every time he went home, his reception in town grew a little cooler, especially after he grew a Joe Namath beard. "Beaver Falls gave *him* a parade."

Stan was talking perched on the corner of my desk this summer. He'd graduated and gone home to serve as an usher at the wedding of a high school classmate from West Point, and was back in New York for a job. Well anyway, it was a nice wedding, and after the ceremony the wedding party and numerous guests all gathered for a reception and dance at the VFW hall. All went well until one of the West Point ushers who is black cut in on a white bridesmaid.

Stan wrote a letter to the editor of the Sherman's Creek *Courier*, printed a few days later, criticizing the town's racism and providing a topic of conversation around the area for weeks. Stan got back his old summer job in a mine but quit because he was called a "nigger lover," and worse.

Stan gazed sadly out my window. One more thing he ought

to add, he said. The friends and acquaintances who stood up for him, including one who had to fight over it, had all—like Stan—attended colleges out of the area: Penn State, Bucknell, Franklin & Marshall. He looked back at me and sighed. "You can't go home again." But he intends to anyway. He's very good working with children. He'll get advanced training for more of that, return to western Pennsylvania to work in Welfare, and go on from that into politics. That's one occupation in which you can change things!

If a high school has a reasonably strong Guidance Office, the counselors probably concentrate heavily on college candidates: in a suburban community steering them toward prestige colleges, in a parochial school toward the colleges of its sect, in smaller towns or the country toward nearby state colleges. The counselors in my home town appear to pressure a large proportion of each graduating class toward the last. They do so partly out of loyalty to the state system, of which most are alumni, but partly too out of loyalty to the local community, which feels threatened by outside influences and new life styles. The counselors hope their students will come back home to live and work without all those foreign ideas. Wouldn't you sometimes almost agree? When Wordsworth wrote "The World Is Too Much With Us," he wished he could become like a primitive person and see things again through unsophisticated eyes. The responsibilities of education and freedom weigh down a person. But the satisfactions he gets from meeting them with a well-developed imagination are heady indeed.

# 9 / Wandering Scholars

*"The food reeks. The townies jump us after dark. I can't follow the mathematics. An epidemic of mono is spreading. One of my roommates snores. The other keeps an owl."*

American college students fritter away a lot of time on campus talking about transferring to other institutions. Apparently they are comforted by the thought that they can pack up and leave at any time—especially if this would disturb the faculty and administration (and sometimes their parents, too). In the end a sizable number actually do transfer: today nearly one entering student in four is a transfer. The total for 1971 should fall between three and four hundred thousand.

These nomads make the academic establishment uncomfortable. They add to our load of paper work and financial worry, for we must refill their places. Also, they offend the moral sense of many who look on them as vagrants. But some educators believe that the student who hits the academic road may be pursuing a sound educational goal.

This vast annual campus reshuffling has several causes. One of them operates even before college. During the admissions procedure, high school seniors are encouraged to apply to several institutions; some apply in pardonable apprehension to as many as fifteen or twenty. Furthermore, they are often urged by their advisers to diversify these college choices—by location, by size, even by type. And the advisers urge this not only as a precaution but sometimes also in hopes that the applicant may select with discrimination, in the manner of a Frenchman choosing a wine!

Note that the parents of these young people, if they went to college, almost all applied to one and only one—and got in. It was easy to stick to such a choice. Nowadays candidates and colleges, at admissions time, are made interchangeable, like industrial parts, and many a candidate finds his college by a sort of lottery. An officer of the College Board described today's admissions procedure as a "system of improvisations in a condition of working obsolescence." Is not so mechanical—and yet chaotic—a process apt to breed the cool transfer student?

Authorities at some colleges suffering heavy transfer out—called "attrition"—say they lie awake nights worrying over the inconvenience of it. But their catalogues usually carry careful instructions to anyone at another college wishing to transfer—in. The faculties of Haverford and Harvard suggested that more of these be accepted. Harvard has had a special application form for them. Some think a transfer is a better risk than a freshman. But do transfers actually improve after switching? Do they get what they want by transferring? How does their shuttling around affect the institutions involved?

In general, no one knows the answers to these questions; so try weighing for yourself the merits of a few cases.

After a couple of years at a West Coast university, a bright young fellow named Ted decides to come East. He can probably hold his scholarship in the process, for his grades are good. He is a political-science major and a fine debater—in fact, visits to other colleges with the debating team seem to have got him thinking about a transfer. So did some congenial Eastern students he ran into in Europe last summer. He would like to see more of New York City. Above all, he says he wants to try a small place where academic give-and-take may be more intimate. In the heart of an apple-and-dairy region within striking distance of Manhattan, he has found just such a college that will accept him.

From there, at the same time, a bright young woman has arranged to transfer West, in order to sit at the feet of a certain eminent philosopher. Sara complains of the intimacy of her small hilltop college, where she says she now knows what everyone will say before they open their mouths. She wants a larger, less personalized community.

Or consider a fellow named Joe. He wasn't doing well at engineering school. With a fine high school record, strong scholastic aptitude, boundless energy, and a desire to learn, he still had a poor record at National Tech. What was the trouble? Simply that he wanted a liberal arts education, while his parents insisted that he get a technical one. ("Be practical, Joe; it's a tough world.") In the end he was allowed to hunt for a liberal arts college. He chose one least like his engineering school, majored in psychology, and now stands on the honors list.

One young man fell ill in his freshman year at Princeton. When he recovered, taking the negative view of his present campus, which is common among freshmen, he transferred to Harvard. This was John F. Kennedy. If he'd stuck it out, Princeton would now have two U.S. Presidents to Harvard's three.

Transfers are found all through the higher-education system. They move from small to large institutions, from a technical curriculum to liberal arts, from strict to free, from country to city, from separate to coed—or the other way. They exchange football for books, dungarees for Bermudas, collegiate life for a part-time job, campus for home—or the reverse. One women's college in a provincial city may lose nearly half its student body per annum; a certain great university takes in as many transfers as freshmen; a small college, of high academic quality but isolated, eventually loses two-thirds of each entering class, but draws enough more from the transfer flow to weather along. Only a few stand like rocks unchanging in the rip of this tide, admitting *no* transfers.

The parents of many of these young people are upset, fearing their children are aimless. But actually they are not so much drifters as seekers.

A young woman went to a college in a small city. It was of good academic reputation, with a tradition of social and intellectual liberalism stemming from the religious group that sponsors it—all proudly asserted in the college catalogue. To her bitter surprise, she found student life dominated by reactionary fraternities and sororities. Such discrepancies between what candidates seek and what they find may be the reason for many transfers. And their persistence in further pursuit of a college degree may be an example of what Dr. Johnson said about the woman who had married for the third time: "Sir, that is the triumph of hope over experience."

Two eminent critics of education defend the colleges for not drawing a more accurate picture of themselves. Professor David Riesman claims that since they are very complex and always changing, there is probably no one on (or off) most campuses able to describe them simply enough to be helpful. Also, he says, parents probably don't *want* to know what a college is really like; they merely want a plausible image of it with which to live comfortably and regale friends and relatives. Professor W. Max Wise, on the other hand, guesses that even if colleges had a clear picture of themselves, most would not publish it for the perfectly honorable reason that they aim to turn into something better.

Meanwhile the students, as adolescents, themselves are growing like the mustard seed; and their growth makes a dramatic leap when they go to college. Fortunate for parents that this miracle takes place away from home! For the first thing the young people do with their new-found critical powers is to train them point-blank on something in the foreground. Of course, this is usually the very college that has helped them most to grow. No matter: the place seems dreadfully imperfect, especially by contrast with old illusions about it. There is nothing new about this: read the words of President Horace Mann, of Antioch College, in his Baccalaureate Sermon for 1857:

A college is a place where character is developed with fearful rapidity. Seeds which might never, or not for years, have germinated at home spring into sudden vitality and shoot up with amazing luxuriance when brought within the active influence of numbers and of institutional excitements. This explains why a College government has a far more arduous task with each of its numerous pupils than a parent with each of his small number of children.

Of course, the students themselves often give their own clear reasons for transferring. Love, money, curriculum, and boredom are frequent pretexts for transfer: to be nearer a girl or boy friend (often, to marry one), to spare a parent's pocketbook, to find more suitable courses, or to escape in genuine dismay the frustration on any campus, the small army of transfers say they pack up and switch colleges. Obviously, such reasons are sometimes crucial: but an admissions officer may catch a whiff of something deeper, probably unknown to the student.

Higher education in the United States has changed its focus from the developing of character to the training of intellect. This refocusing of purpose has produced a new attitude: students feel less attachment to their campus.

The academic work at our earlier colleges was easy and quite unscholarly by today's standards. Their goal was to "make men," as Mark Hopkins of Williams College put it. In fact, this famous educator was proudly anti-intellectual and aimed to offer, first of all, hearty moral leadership. In those character-building days students transferred, but not often. We wanted young people to remain bound in simple loyalty to each other and to a campus. I'm just old enough to have seen a cane rush. From opposite ends of a football field, the freshmen and the sophomores swarmed to possess a prize cane for which two of their leaders had begun to tussle at the fifty-yard line. To a small boy the melee was fascinating, if terrifying. To the collegians involved, it added another link in the chain of intense experiences tying them to Alma Mater.

Today the leading colleges, after a 100-year struggle against the old collegiate tradition, are now devoted, at least officially, to "making *minds*." The faculty are offering much richer studies and demanding harder work; and the undergraduates are increasingly preoccupied with preparation for graduate school.

The football at more and more colleges is the despair of old grads and the amiable mockery of sports writers. I asked a sophomore to tell me who goes to the rallies these days. "Quite frankly," he replied, "nobody I know has ever been near one." But he talked eagerly of his plan to "cover" the nearby art museum in order to enjoy his humanities course more this year.

Even when I was a college student forty years ago a titan from the Class of 1902 clutched my lapels in tragic passion on the porch of a summer hotel as he begged me to explain why the old spirit had disappeared from campus. If still alive, what would he think of the students in an old, top-ranking men's college where two-thirds of the sophomore class, in a campus survey, said they had thought of transferring? One fifth said they had even gone so far as to inquire into transfer possibilities. These cavalier young men would have been disowned by his generation, who would have offered you their right arm, torn off at the socket, rather than go to another college. Imagine their scorn for the sophomore who last year explained why he had *not* thought of such a thing: "My reasons? Inertia, and a certain satisfaction with the place. I guess I like it."

But the students' detachment has not yet changed the conventional official view of transfer: it is unfavorable. To many deans and registrars this drifting still seems inefficient and even a little immoral. A student ought to attend only one college for his bachelor's degree: he should choose wisely and stay. This pristine view was stated by a professor in a college newspaper: "In my day it did not occur to us, when unhappy, to withdraw from college to 'find ourselves.' We were inclined, rather, to stay put till we had made something out of ourselves worth finding."

Also, our unfavorable attitude toward transfer may stem from the old sectarianism in our colleges, most of which were founded by religious sects to protect the souls of young members. When religion lost its extreme fervor in the last century and football took its place as the focus of higher education, bitter gridiron rivalries helped perpetuate a sense of the exclusiveness of one's college. To go elsewhere still seemed like a sin.

This attitude, well disguised, still may affect the parents' and faculties' view of transfer.

Officialdom may look negatively on transfers simply because it finds them embarrassing. Except for those from two-year colleges (between a quarter and a third of the whole group), their movement implies a criticism: of the place they have left, for not satisfying them; of the place they go to next, for taking in academic flotsam.

Then what, for example, is your own opinion of this case? A young man applied for his *sixth* transfer from one liberal arts college to another. The admissions officer at college number six exerted himself to size this fellow up cautiously. But he turned out to be an otherwise impeccable candidate: well recommended all around, not critical of the colleges he left behind, grateful, in fact, for the learning he had acquired during each sojourn, and eager for the special advantages of the college of his newest choice. Would you admit him? Is he an academic tramp, selfishly, even neurotically exploiting the colleges, or is he a free citizen of the Republic of Learning using his passport for profitable travel?

He may have been led on by the same spirit of eclecticism that used to keep German students on the move. Abraham Flexner, the great educational administrator and critic, did not think much of U.S. higher education. He even thought the British pretty callow. But he greatly admired the German, and one feature of German univerisities that impressed him was the constant transferring on the part of the students. This is how he weighed the merits of this custom in *Universities, American, English, German:*

The loyalty which marks the Harvard man in the United States, the Oxford man in England, is unknown in Germany, except perhaps to the extent of a sentimental attachment to the university in which the student spent his first semester. There is no such thing as a Greifswald man, a Vienna man, a Berlin man. Unquestionably, this indifference is costly; it costs some of the personal and institutional attachments that add to the amenities of life in English-speaking countries. . . . Nonetheless . . . intellectually the German gains far more than he loses through wandering. It has its disadvantages: for example, it enables an indifferent student to seek his degree wherever it is more easily obtained. But what is more important, it enables the able student to go where his subject is most vigorously prosecuted, and it stimulates the professor to do his best in order to attract the most competent students; for on the quality of his students depend the fame of seminar and laboratory and to some extent the professor's income.

The Junior Year Abroad has long been considered good for some students. Now a number of colleges are planning to suggest foreign study for all. May this not simply be the further burgeoning of the domestic transfer movement? The University of Kansas faculty once asked the state legislature for funds to assist any of their liberal arts students to go abroad for a year of study to count toward the degree. Might not the faculty consider it nearly as good and far less expensive to urge students to take a year in a college in another part of the U.S.A.?

Perhaps modern young people would benefit from such systematic migration as much as the wandering scholars did in Aquinas's day, according to those words of a medieval monk, quoted in Paul Monroe's great *Textbook in the History of Education*:

The scholars are accustomed to wander throughout the whole world and visit all the cities; and their many studies bring them understanding. For in Paris they seek a knowledge of the liberal arts; of the ancient writers at Orléans; of medicine at Salernum; of the black art at Toledo.

Is our geographic mobility as a nation a permanent habit? If so, some academic mobility probably must go with it. If, in addition, transfer had educational value in itself, our wandering scholars could be a rich asset, not only bettering their own studies but cross-fertilizing the academic garden.

But hold on. William James used to advise a person contemplating suicide: wait for the next mail. A college student contemplating transfer might well wait until the next semester. He certainly shouldn't make the decision if it's bad weather, or shortly before or during an exam period, or if long term papers are pressing him. And he should be wary of any such drastic move during his "sophomore slump." Not everyone suffers one, and some suffer it at other stages of education—one person I know, for example, insists he went through it in the fourth grade. But even the sophomore in his identity crisis will see the winter slush disappear. He may discover an electrifying professor, or a girl, or himself, and be glad he stayed around.

My last word about transfer is addressed to young people dropping out of our colleges. In some, the rate is said to be going up. A Dean at Harvard, in February, 1971, spoke of 300 leaves of absence this year, double the average for several recent years. He suggested it is "a reflection of the disparity between what students are sorting out for themselves and what the University can offer them to solve their problems." A student put it more strongly, speaking, he said, for many of those taking leave. "Not only are the courses here irrelevant; they are just plain harmful. They teach an entirely perverted way of thinking, a way which exists solely for the preservation of the social system."

Whether taking leave or dropping out, college students, however negative about present education, should know of the strong evidence that they will probably return or go elsewhere to finish. The last estimate I saw revealed that about half the degree students in all U.S. higher education were over twenty-five years old. And an Arizona university, which once traced all its former students, found some still graduating, there or elsewhere, twenty-five or thirty years after they had entered.

Nationally, a little more than one-quarter of those who go to college do not get a degree—ever. But if they spend at least a semester on most campuses, and if they haven't been thrown out too embarrassingly, colleges will consider them alumni with some or all of these advantages: listing in the alumni directory with the class in which they started; invitation to class reunions; a place in the academic procession at commencements; football seats near the fifty-yard line; and—you can be pretty sure—the opportunity to contribute to alumni fund drives. A certain successful advertsising man, who transferred from Duke to Columbia and then dropped out for good, is allowed these privileges by both institutions.

# 10 / Countercurriculum

*Among his other wise sayings, Aristotle remarked that man is by nature a social animal; and it is in order to develop his powers as a social being that American colleges exist.*

—ABBOTT LAWRENCE LOWELL,
President of Harvard
Inaugural Address, 1909

Old fashioned collegiate spirit is dying on many of our campuses. On some, the band is one of its last preserves—especially the tomfoolery. Bandsmen, passing through a rival college town on an overnight trip, are still known to pile out of their buses in the small hours to play football songs under dormitory windows—fortissimo. The old spirit is also supposed to survive in fraternities. Invented a century and a half ago to promote fellowship and freedom, they were a student revolution against open puritanism. The fraternities are said to be declining. This could not be because puritanism is dead. It is only less open. Nor is the compensatory need for brotherhood and intimacy on campus declining. Probably youth needs newer forms than the fraternity for self-protection and self-expression.

Other traditional extracurricular activities are declining—varsity sports, musical clubs, proms, debating, class offices—as youth questions the traditional life and work for which these are a sort of preparation. Such activities are too formal, too official. Worst of all, they are desired and supported by the university.

But a new kind of campus activity is emerging that can help prepare young people for untraditional tasks. These tasks require a very personal and independent but limited sort of relationship. Not that an American does not need and get deep and lasting friendship as much as ever. I disagree with pessimists who lament that this gift is disappearing here. I believe it never was as common anywhere as they think. Did Hamlet have any real friends besides Horatio to lodge in his heart's core, ay, in his heart of heart? Life and work in this country has always required relationships that are warm but fugitive. Groups of us have been coming together for an urgent but short-range purpose: a pioneer wagon train, a log raising, a P-TA committee, a block council, a political or professional task force, an industrial production team, a moonshot. These tasks usually call for shifting, informal leadership and easy communication, rapport, and interdependence—relationships that are quick and warm but not so deep that we will feel frustrated at parting. We are like knights-errant falling in together to drive an ogre from his castle. We converge from here or there; we disperse when the job is done, probably never to meet again. In the emerging world order called "technetronic" by Zbigniew Brzezinski, this skill may be more important than ever.

College undergraduates are anticipating this style of functioning by inventing new organizations and projects of their own. The university authorities are usually indifferent if not reluctant. This substitute for the dying extracurriculum, or cocurriculum, might be called the "countercurriculum." It may be a more important confrontation than the more publicized confrontation of violence.

The trend is obvious in athletics. The nineteenth-century athlete invented and promoted our now familiar team sports, at first against official opposition. In the 1870's, when the Cor-

nell men asked President Andrew Dickson White for permission
to meet Michigan in Cleveland for a football game, he refused
it. "I see no advantage," he grumbled, "in two dozen young men
traveling four hundred miles to agitate a leather object inflated
with air." But soon officialdom took over. Now, again, like his
ancestor, today's athlete is eagerly introducing his own sport.
Student-sponsored rugby has been booming to the point that
college athletic authorities felt threatened by the drain on
varsity manpower. It's hard, honorable work to serve as captain
or manager of an established varsity sport. But it's an exercise in
creative human relations to help start one where there was none,
getting out a newsletter about it, dunning some parents and
alumni for funds, agreeing on a uniform, and keeping one another's spirits up during the first losing seasons. I've seen
Columbia students introduce sailing and hockey this way. And
what if you're starting up an eccentric sport, like flying or rodeo,
or a heroic one, like mountain climbing or spelunking?

At Guilford, a Quaker college in North Carolina, some
students were unsatisfied by the regular religious service conducted by a college official, with sermon, hymns, and formal
prayers. They wanted to worship in the old Quaker way, everyone his own minister, communicating in silence. So they liberated the college worship. They organized their own Sunday
silent meeting, where they met to share the silence and one another's thoughts if moved to speak. Though faculty and administrators at first objected to this challenge, a number soon
started to take part in the silent meetings.

Across the hall from my office at Columbia the student-run
Draft Information Center seethes with activity all day and far
into the evening. Nothing has ever confused college students
more than a recruiting system many of them judge unfair for a
war they abhor. Yet, in general, faculty and administrators have
neglected their confusion. And the national associations of
college counselors have been ignoring draft counseling. So on a
number of campuses students counsel each other. At Columbia,
since the fall of 1967, an over-all total of about 100 student
volunteers have been training each other in the counseling of
more than 7,000 young men anxious and more or less ignorant

about their legal rights and responsibilities. The advice is said to be as technically sound as any available anywhere. The attitude of the university authorities toward the program ranged from hostile to lukewarm. One academic-department chairman refused to let his younger instructors participate. "Keep your cottonpickin' hands off them," he warned its director. "You'd only delay their doctoral theses."

Before pollution hit the headlines, some other Columbia students were throwing themselves into an efficient campaign to educate the local population in the facts and theory that bear on environmental protection. At that time the curriculum offered virtually nothing in ecological studies. The science faculty, the most competent to help fight the social crimes of pollution, seemed indifferent to them. But the students organized a speakers' bureau, a bulletin, and a course of study. I knew one of the workers, a Ph.D. candidate in Chinese studies. Ed was giving talks on ecology to citizens' groups in both the city and the suburbs.

The effect of this experience upon this young man was profound. He may be representative. Ed is brilliant, warmhearted, and responsible. He joined in the occupation of one of our buildings in the troubles of Spring, 1968, striving together with hundreds of others to mediate between the Leninist leaders of the revolt and our baffled administrators and faculty. He insists poor human communication is one of the worst forms of pollution.

After seeing frenzied policemen blackjack his friends, Ed decided to give up his Ph.D. program. He came to me for advice about getting a job in some corporation like IBM, where he could learn modern management techniques while seeing if an industrial organization is more open to change than a university. After interviews with a number of executives, Ed changed his strategy. He and his wife are now living and working quietly in a small, poor Virginia town, soliciting a trickle of cash from their New York friends and relations to help the neighbors organize to improve their lot.

Ed's generation wants to triumph over inertia. I caught a hint of its power to do this at a conference of the Eastern

College Placement Officers a couple of years ago. I was chatting at the clambake with the Dean of Western New England College. "Has the revolution hit your campus?" I asked. Not yet. They enroll a pretty conservative set of students. Many are business and technical majors earnestly preparing themselves for work in the Springfield area. Come to think of it, though, there'd been one incident maybe with revolutionary implications. One morning, before the administrators arrived for work, a five-ton boulder had been transported from somewhere and neatly placed so as to block the front entrance of their building. The Dean, who is respected, had been tipped off the night before and told not to worry. No message, no explanation. After the next night, the great granite obstacle was gone.

Hearing this account by the Dean, I recalled the archaeologists' astonishment that the builders of the Pharaohs and the Mayans, even with slaves, could have hoisted stones of such size. Yet at Western New England it was done with participatory democracy.

Since then that boulder has often rolled into my mind. It seems to promise that today's young people will be undertaking things my generation has dismissed as hopeless. They seem ready to change things and be changed. The youth revolution has created new styles of dress and conduct for a large majority; affluence has rid many of them of the prudence required of their parents; countless hours of rock songs, with their fierce or tender lyrics, have sensitized them spiritually; civil-rights conflict, unpopular war, and assassinations have deepened their concern. And why are so many of them steeped in science fiction? Only recently have a few English departments offered a course in this serious literature. But some college bookstores display up to fifty or sixty feet of it on their shelves. At its best it is beautiful; it is coming true. Perhaps that is why people who have read it avidly may feel more ready to struggle for the realization of man's dreams.

Another hint for optimists can be picked up in college bookstores. In a recent issue, the new magazine of higher education, *Change*, reported the best sellers on their shelves. The latest sampling was from Stanford, Utah, Wyoming, and Ohio State universities and from Bowdoin College. There, J. R. R. Tolkien's books of fantasy were still moving briskly. His Hobbits help students keep their minds off the Mess. They're also reading about animals in Robert Ardrey's *The Territorial Imperative* and Desmond Morris's *The Naked Ape.* There they are assured that the Mess is caused by man's animal traits. But another title has intruded: *The Peter Principle,* about why things always go wrong. This book suggests in addition how to make them go right. Could it be that, like Ed, students want help in developing their bent for co-operative action? Robert Townsend's *Up the Organization* should be on the next college best-seller list. It is, quite literally, an ABC of how to use Participatory Democracy in a corporation.

I observed its use by young people at the Washington peace rally in May, 1970. A hundred thousand of them, with only a few days' notice, converged from two dozen states to commune for several hours and then depart. They maintained their vitality during a long ceremony in above-ninety-degree heat. A large staff of smiling student marshals directed the crowd. Such good order prevailed that the police used tear gas only once or twice. And those who provoked the tear gas pained the others more than I'd expected. "Some of us blew it," lamented a knot of Ohio students with whom I talked by the Washington Monument. "It was beautiful and we blew it." We. One of them wore a Kent State shirt. When I looked at the name, he apologized. "Actually I go to Youngstown—but it's only thirty miles away."

The rally was rated a failure by many participants. The government apparently ignored it. "And we'd heard all those speeches before." So had I. But the event was a repetition of an extraordinary new accomplishment. They had used again, as in the McCarthy campaign in New Hampshire and at Woodstock, a skill in fast, massive, orderly, constructive action demonstrated by no earlier generation of American young people.

As Fletcher Pratt wrote in his *Short History of the Civil War,* the Northern officers and soldiers at the Battle of Gettysburg would not have cared to know that they were winning with a new method. They just wanted to win. This they did, by relying less on staff generalship, more on small field decisions, than soldiers had in any major battle in history. Ever since, Pratt believes, the American people have continued to function in government, industry, and politics with this freer, more democratic, but effective style. Given an over-all plan, we do not rely so much on leaders.

Doesn't this skill help account for some of the success of the youth movement? It was evident long before recent events. On a smaller scale, black college students in the lunch-counter and restaurant sit-ins of the early 1960's were mounting a loose but systematic campaign. It was strong enough to draw in one young black who was the first at a certain Southern white women's college. The sit-in movement was now visible. When a resentful white spilled a bowl of piping hot soup down her back in the college dining hall, she went off and joined up. Then the Northern students who traveled South to promote civil rights stepped up the campaign with the same sort of organizational style. Those middle-class white idealists were terrified of the sheriffs and rednecks. "When we drove over lonely roads, we never knew who might be in the next car." But feeling the strength of a network of their fellows, they dared to keep on.

Doesn't this skill account for the success of the web of programs like the Youth Emergency Service, by which young people take care of each other systematically in their quest to get away from the system? One Eastern student recognized the YES arm band on a young person in a bus terminal in Minneapolis. YES offered him a pad, a meal, medical or legal help, or a clergyman. He says the clergy are helpful because the police cannot require them to share confidences.

"Then go ahead and call us good organizers," conceded another student, "but not just us Americans." At the rock festival on the Isle of Wight in the summer of 1970, he pointed out, $6,000 bail money was collected through an organization made up on the spot. "Ten minutes after they busted you, you were listening to music again."

Though our educational, governmental, and industrial systems are more flexible than those of any other large nation, they still resist improvement stubbornly. But I doubt that all their defenses can hold firm against the oncoming cohorts of a generation mellowed by the fantasists, inspired by the science-fiction classics, sobered by anthropological pessimists, instructed by administrative radicals, and already experienced on campus and through their own continental subculture in new techniques of group and mass action.

# 11 / Women

*If we make them our equals, they will soon be our masters.*

—CATO THE ELDER

In the 1880's my grandfather went to Germany on a sabbatical leave from Haverford College to do research at the University of Berlin. Accompanying him, my grandmother, a scholar, a writer, and a beauty, became the first coed in Germany. She applied for admission to a course at the university. No women had ever been admitted, they insisted, or ever could be. My grandfather leaned gently on a bureaucrat or two until they allowed her to enroll. They hid her from the other students behind a screen.

Why did my grandmother dare to stand up to a German university? Perhaps because she was a member of the Society of Friends, that sect which had given up most distinctions between men and women, even the titles Mr. and Mrs., as long ago as the seventeenth century. She was a relative of Lucretia Mott, the Quaker champion of women's rights. And she could see the brisk progress in the battle for coeducation in America.

Both Oberlin and Antioch colleges, founded in Ohio in 1833 and 1852, began as coeducational institutions. They soon enjoyed such heavy enrollment that they embarrassed all the men's colleges, which were hard up as usual for students. Many young progressives braved it there from the East Coast, traveling by canalboat if they were still anxious about riding in "the cars."

Admission of women kept pace with the rapid growth of our Western colleges and universities. Coeducation was expedient as an alternative to the costly dual system. It seemed educationally sound to introduce a gentler female element into the harsh life of the segregated male collegian. In a legislative hearing over the admission of women to one Midwestern college, the janitor of another testified that after the enrollment of women, he found the men less often wrestling in the halls and spitting on the floor.

The South and East resisted coeducation for a long time by setting up separate and unequal colleges for women. Wellesley was the first college to offer laboratory science to women, but Wellesley students of those early days were preparing mainly to become schoolteachers or wives of missionaries. On the other hand, M. Carey Thomas, President of Bryn Mawr from 1894 to 1922, may have advocated too aggressive a feminism. She created a pioneer program of doctoral studies comparable to the best for men. And her alumnae were said to have felt guilty when they "only married," in Miss Thomas's disdainful words.

Against heavy odds, a few male champions fought for coeducation in the East. President F. A. P. Barnard tried to establish a women's division at Columbia but was defeated by faculty, alumni, and students. Later, one emerged as a separate but affiliated branch and was given Barnard's name. This compromise—the co-ordinate women's college—was a devious defense put up by several distinguished Eastern men's colleges. A grudging concession to women's education, it kept the coeds at arm's length. The co-ordinate-women's-college catalogue fea-

tured its closeness to men. The men's catalogue barely mentioned the women. Historian Frederick Rudolph notes that it
is metaphorically confusing to describe Columbia, Harvard, and
Tufts as giving birth to Barnard, Radcliffe, and Jackson. He
suggests that we refer to the co-ordinate college instead as
"Adam's rib."

But the war for equal status in the men's academic world was
finally won by the young women themselves. They simply went
in and stayed there until their presence was formally recognized.

They were recognized first by young men who needed them.
An editor of the college paper at Furman University, in South
Carolina, insisted he learned most at college from two years
with a bright roommate who spent much of the time trying to
decide whether or not life was worth living. Helping his roommate face this enigma challenged more of Bob's capabilities
than satisfying the academic requirements of the Furman
faculty. Was the roommate suicidal? Well, his doubts were
more than philosophical but maybe less than psychotic. How
were they resolved? In the spring of junior year, his roommate's
existential anxiety subsided when the yellow jasmine appeared
and he fell in love with a Furman girl.

During the 1940's, the "library date" was spreading among
the men and women in coeducational or neighboring sexually
segregated colleges. Couples thought that together they could
do their homework better. Side by side in the reading room,
they resembled Paul and Francesca, Dante's two young lovers,
united by their longing for each other and by a poetic old book.
My guess is that many thousands, potential dropouts from
frustration or failure, were kept in college by romance.

Nowadays, even more such rescues may take place in the
colleges that let the sexes come together in their dormitory
rooms or in off-campus apartments. A great many young people
make much of this privilege as a chance to study together. He
may be doing his philosophy, she her physics. They don't talk
much. Now and then one says, "What do you suppose this
means?" or "Here's something cool. . . ."

During the 1950's, when the band rode to distant football
games, the bandsmen's women friends were coming along in

the buses. And when asked why his men no longer indulged in the nearly annual spring riot, the Dean of Harvard gave as one reason that their companions from nearby women's colleges got in the way. Women were only a step from their full participation in today's campus confrontations, at which their clear, high voices command even more attention than the men's.

My mother was disconcerted to find that an undergraduate who lived with her in the early 1960's as a part-time helper kept some of her dresses in her boy-friend's Harvard dormitory closet. Many people were disconcerted a year or two ago when the morning papers, covering a bomb scare that emptied one of Columbia's dorms in the small hours, reported that a sizable number of young women in pajamas rushed out along with the men. And millions read *Life*'s picture article in November, 1970, about the newly established coeducational dormitories at Oberlin, where the students make their own decisions about their living arrangements. This is a college run by high-pressure, academically conservative, but still socially creative educators. They hold to the fiercely independent tradition of their founders, who admitted women and blacks from the start and permitted the college to become a station on the Underground Railroad, where armed students stood off U.S. marshals pursuing runaway slaves. Much of respectable America was as scandalized then as now. *Life* printed a letter from an Indiana woman asking how long the Lord will withhold His wrath from Oberlin. But in another letter an official of the national YMCA politely pointed out that its George Williams College, near Chicago, had set up coed dormitories thirty years ago, "where young men and young women could live with and see each other as just people with all their strengths and weaknesses."

The skirmishes, the diversions, the infiltrations of the young women, have finally led to victory and conquest. The strongest pockets of resistance, our old Eastern men's colleges, began surrendering in the 1960's. Remote hilltop retreats like Hamilton and Colgate, ancient male fastnessess like Princeton and Yale, have gone or are going coeducational. During the last few years, each capitulation has been reported in the papers as though it were Vicksburg or Khartoum. The most spectacular collapse was Fordham's. From the beginning, students at Roman Catholic colleges in America have been the most strictly segregated. The news that it was all over at the Bronx campus appeared in a New York paper under a front-page headline: THEY'RE IN AT LAST.

Like the first attempts, this final triumph of coeducation cannot be attributed to enlightened educational leadership. On the contrary, it must be attributed to economic expedience and the formalization of a *fait accompli* for which the students deserve the credit. As usual, educators dress up their pragmatism with rhetoric about progress and the needs of youth.

Several serious questions remain about the education of women and of men. Separatists such as Lynn White, Jr., President of Mills College in California, have still been protesting. In 1950, in his book *Educating Our Daughters*, he argued that women can be educated better among women. With men around, he alleged, a coed cannot be so much herself, as a student or as a person. Above all, he warned, she will hold back academically lest she appear too intellectually formidable to the men. She may see an unmistakable fallacy in Guglielmo Ferrero's theory of the legitimacy of political power. But if in a class discussion she spoke up about it, President White warned that the men in the room would feel turned off by her. Either they'd be jealous that they didn't think of it themselves, or afraid that she might redirect her critical aim from Ferrero to them.

Others have regretted seeing a young man miss the old-fashioned brotherly collegiate whirl. He meets a woman in his freshman year, and they become firmly attached. Together they avoid most traditional campus activities. During the decade of the 1950's this informal monogamy was becoming popular at Bard College. A professor there spoke of it with despair. How could men understand women if they knew only one? As a student in the 1930's at Kenyon, not then coed, he had dated fifty-six different girls in one academic year. Where he found them in a small town fifty miles north of Columbus I forgot to ask. But whoever they were, he insists they provided a valuable part of his education.

Obviously they also protected him from the challenge of intimacy. Who is to say how long young American men and women should be protected from each other? And how much can we criticize them for immature conduct in an experience where they have not been given the responsibility that alone brings maturity?

They expressed their frustration over that injustice after I talked on a college radio program about the topic "College Students: Angels or Monsters?"—monsters, that is, in the medical sense: distorted, incomplete, unnatural. The title of the talk was mine. As I moved to the mike, I thought of that unseen crowd of listeners whom we educator's alternately call "young adults" or "late adolescents." They never can be sure which we take them for. So I apologized for our vacillation and for our consequent unfairness in depriving them of most responsibilities—civic, financial, domestic, sexual, professional, and (often) military—and then loading them down with the least maturing and often most stultifying kind of responsibility —academic. In this way we make monsters out of our young people. Then we complain because their conduct is not angelic.

I feared the monster image might have been too strong. But when I stopped in at the coffee shop after the broadcast and found a crowd who had listened to it, they were cheerfully calling each other monsters. They liked the term. It described how they felt, especially, they said, about sex. They're supposed to act as though they had none. "I'm a monster," cried out a lovely person named Nina, and tried to twist herself into an ugly contortion.

Ten years ago, some college psychiatrists were dubious about the growing tendency toward premature intimacy between college men and women, premature, that is, in the eyes of traditionalists. It's just because we deprive them of other maturing experiences, one psychiatrist explained to me, that they are all the less able to cope with this big experience. It needs to be balanced by others, like work, or children, or some important service. Academic study, which is solitary and too often emotionally shallow, does not balance it. It can even aggravate the imbalance.

I know of no recent psychiatric consensus about the harm or good in the now even further advanced intimacy among our students. They contend that in their freedom and earnestness they are less promiscuous than earlier generations. How they know the difference, let alone measure it, they don't say.

One sophomore came for information about a full-time job. I asked Al how he'd find time. Oh, it wasn't for him; it was for his girl. I reminded him she was in Syracuse. That's right, but, like, she's coming to the city. To the city. Oh. For a visit? No. Like, to live. "I've got to have her near me."

I haven't yet learned one lesson these affectionate young people are teaching. Our higher education is so unbearable to a large proportion of them that they need extraordinary protection from its threats. Love may be a better defense than drugs or violence.

# 12 / Blacks

*Somewhere in the early-nineteenth-century annals of Harvard: The college has just accepted a black for admission. His name is Beverly Williams. A group of busybodies descends on President Edward Everett to warn that if the young black enters, the students will all resign. "In that case, gentlemen, the entire resources of the university will be devoted to the education of Mr. Williams."*

Fifty years ago, on the way to school I used to walk through Preston, a black ghetto next to our Philadelphia suburb. A certain small boy would sometimes rush out and challenge me to fight. He knew his rights, he declared. I had done nothing to provoke him that I was aware of, except walk past. But maybe that was enough.

There were no blacks in my elementary or high school. I recall only one in college in the early 1930's—a fellow classics major named Frank Snowden. We were nodding acquaintances. I admired him and perhaps also resented him a little because he was always perfectly prepared in class. Yet he did not alter my conception of blacks as gracious, deferent, hard-working people, a few of whom can be unaccountably edgy. Maybe I refrained from getting to know Frank better for fear he would start talking about his rights. Twenty years later, as a commencement aide, I was to hand to a college president the diploma and hood for an honorary LL.D., which was to be conferred upon Frank Snowden, then a distinguished diplomat. He had grown a mustache; he was as handsome as ever, and friendly.

In the early 1960's the few blacks at Columbia were likely to be well qualified in grades, test scores, family (usually professional), and consequent intellectual sophistication. They tended to do well for two or three years. Then that big question came into the back of their minds: Can I really make it in the white world? If I do not, won't I be all the more humiliated just because I have a good college degree? Isn't that degree beginning to look more like a threat than a blessing? Some whites of humble origin who get to Ivy League colleges feel this same compunction. The blacks have felt it more keenly because of the color of their skin. In junior and senior year, large proportions of them were falling into academic difficulties.

A few were coming in for advice concerning work, usually a job for a year or so while they resolved their dilemma. Then, in the later 1960's, they stopped suddenly. At about that time, the Dean was upset by a meeting he'd had with the college's two dozen blacks (out of 2,500). He'd always talked with them one by one. They'd been amiable and—he thought—grateful for his interest. Not now, not together. One after another they denounced the univeristy as racist—deans, faculty, students, curriculum, community. All this poured out in an angry group tirade, said the Dean, holding out his arms in a gesture of surprise and despair.

Blacks ceased coming to our office for a few years. The ethnic gap, wide all along, became impassable. We could measure it when the college's humor magazine printed one well-meant but ill-conceived joke about blacks. In response, a party of black students broke into the office of *Jester*, took away the entire issue by force, and hid it. They then negotiated about improvements in the university's resources for blacks, including the appointment of a dean of their own color.

The gap was revealed even more dramatically in 1968 when

our black students rejected the whites from partnership in the occupation of Hamilton Hall. "Are you cats ready to die in this confrontation? Tomorrow? Today?" they asked. The answer was an exodus of the Students for a Democratic Society to take over another university building.

At this point, the blacks appeared to have turned off in all their relations with the university except for the necessary minimum to stay in and get their degree. With an upsurge in their sense of identity, the brothers and sisters decided to get advice from each other or from older blacks. The reason was partly for solidarity, partly because they'd discovered white advice can do a black more harm than good.

Those last two notions were behind the reactions of two freshmen this year. I'm the adviser of the first. Carter is soft-voiced and good-looking—Michelangelo would have used him for a black "David." He was a flanker on the freshman football team. He assures me everything's okay. So I described to Carter a deep and delicate problem an older white student faced last year in his personal life. Since I was his adviser, he had turned to me to discuss it. If he, Carter, needed help with a big personal problem like that one, would he turn to me? He said he would not. Why not? Because he wouldn't want to show a white person that he was in trouble. What's so wrong about that? It would justify the whites' contempt for his people.

The other black freshman came in the door for advice about planning his academic program for the next three years so it would provide the best preparation for a career. "Where I come from there are only three: minister, teacher, janitor." Robert was the first black freshman in a couple of years who had turned to my office for help. He had no academic major or occupation in mind. He wanted to decide on both now.

What subject had he enjoyed the most? Wouldn't it be better to design an academic program around that? Why not hang loose for a while? After all, the liberal arts college was originally supposed to be a haven for leisurely growth. I talked with Robert as I often do with middle-class whites who are under excessive pressure from insecure parents. I explained the old-fashioned paradox that some can prepare themselves best by preparing themselves least. Robert seemed interested. He discussed the topic logically. I asked what he'd gotten from the discussion. Nothing, he said. That may be a good idea for some whites, but a black doesn't have that kind of time. A black starts too far behind. If he hangs loose, man, he's dead. Robert drew an imaginary knife across his throat.

Black college students are often puritans. When asked to research their own lives, focusing on what they've enjoyed doing, they balk. Only one has ever used our method of functional self-analysis, described in Chapter 18. Black college students are wary of examining what they've enjoyed. They feel more like examining what they ought to do. Their resources seem too limited for anything else; their sense of responsibility is too keen—a responsibility greater than any felt by the most strenuous young whites. For the blacks must use their opportunity in college to better not only themselves but their people. This responsibility has too often fallen on young black students as a burden—"Out of so many millions, why have I been chosen? Am I capable of the mission?" Unsure of themselves, they were often dropping out of college or floundering in an early career.

Because of this sense of urgency, young blacks have attacked head on the academic curriculum in its obsolescence. A decade ago, through their Southern-restaurant sit-ins, black college students attracted the country's attention to basic civil rights. Now, through their occupation of college buildings, demanding studies that make sense to them, they have attracted attention to basic academic rights. Black college students have thus served as shock troops in the first modern effective assault on both civic and academic Bourbonism. The black studies they have demanded include the essential elements needed in white studies: an emphasis on urgent social rather than scholastic problems; teaching suited to students' readiness; new kinds of teachers, including, if necessary, uncertified ones; and admissions directed toward helping rather than screening our youth.

White militant students have mostly side-stepped these issues. Despairing of reform of the college's regular curriculum, they have created their own countercurriculum. Blacks have been more bold. They have aimed to reform the regular studies directly and at once. They have not spent their energies improvising, on their own, escapes from it, however creative. More aware than whites of the irrelevance of today's college program because more handicapped by it, they have insisted not that it be revised but scrapped and replaced. Many educators dismiss the proposal of black studies as a deviation that would take young blacks out of the mainstream of U.S. higher education. Black studies, on the contrary, point out the direction in which the mainstream must be rechanneled, away from the exclusive interests of the scholar and his young protoprofessionals and toward the education of young people for more meaningful living.

My impression is that blacks at Columbia today are not suffering the syndrome so familiar among them in the early 1960's. I don't believe they quietly fizzle out toward the end as students and as persons.

Truman, a freshman from Mississippi, works in my office. One day he thought a member of the staff had called him "boy" with condescension. I guess I convinced Truman he was mistaken. Even so, he refused to work for, or even near that person again. He probably won't ever do any slow or unobtrusive collapsing. He will explode, like his Afro, and go. Or he will stay and get what he wants.

A couple of years ago three seniors at an Ivy League college formed an organization to help fellow black students get what they want. They named it "Operation Cornerstone." Their aim was to raise money for scholarships, gather information about careers in big business, and bring black students into personal contact with successful whites. The scholarships will secure the indispensable degree, the big-business information will lead them to the places where power lies, the contacts will show them how it is wielded. Lacking power figures in their family or neighborhood, they say this last function of Operation Cornerstone is critical. They need an intimate view of white style. "We are not interested in how to become Thirty-second Vice-President and House Nigger."

They consider the white establishment corrupt but far from rotten. "It's dirty, but tough, and it's not about to cave in." So they'll try to get into it, learn its secrets, and ask to be advanced on merit. What if they're not? Ah, for that eventuality they're ready too. What'll they do? They'll do—what they'll do. No further comment.

Operation Cornerstone began with several dinners on campus, each for a dozen black students and a figure or two from their university's upper hierarchy—drinks and roast beef in a private room at the Faculty Club. The evenings were most enjoyable. The university worthies were pleased, even flattered. What else did the students get out of the dinners? A much better sense of what those cats are really like.

Money for the program? The university bureaucracy considered Operation Cornerstone a bunch of operators (wrongly) and said no. The fellows then got to the President. Convinced (rightly) that their purpose was integrationist, not separatist, he gave them what they needed. Operation Cornerstone then planned an intercollegiate conference for black students. It was to present to them a group of successful black businessmen, none Thirty-second Vice-Presidents, for a look-see and dialogue. One difficulty: the same bureaucracy was convinced that Operation Cornerstone leaders were phony and the conference a chimera. Again, the leaders got to the President. Another difficulty: if the campus chapter of the separatist Student Afro-American Society got wind of an integrationist conference, trouble probably, possibly violence.

Result: over 200 students came from over 100 colleges for a flawless day-long conference with a dozen businessmen and an evening rock party. Incredibly, SAS did not know of the affair until the next day.

I've met some of the staff of Operation Cornerstone and talked at length with one of its leaders. A hero of David's is Machiavelli, especially as interpreted in Antony Jay's *Management and Machiavelli*. So I was surprised to find that he hadn't read Clausewitz. When I quoted in German the only maxim I remember from *The Art of War*, "*Wenn Sie nicht zurückgehen, so geht der Feind zurück*," David translated it back at once: "If you don't retreat, the enemy will retreat." He whipped out his notebook and wrote down the German.

As the Chairman of the Board of Trustees took that academic hood from the President and was slipping it over Frank Snowden's head, I mused that the honorary degree can be a good defensive weapon. Like Dr. King's Nobel Prize, it saves us whites the trouble of really helping the blacks. Every time an honor is conferred on an outstanding black, hundreds, thousands, even millions of whites relax. Now we can put off till tomorrow persuading some union to admit more blacks to their ranks or acting in a serious and practical way to make "fair housing" a reality in city and suburb.

We whites do have a tender conscience, which we soothe when we can by doing something easy. Electing a black as student-body president can be another such palliative. Today's New York *Times* reports that the students of Vanderbilt, a predominantly white Southern university, have just elected Larry Wallace, a black, to be their president. Wallace received 744 votes to the 216 of his nearest rival.

Which will advance our civilization more: the expiatory rituals of decent young whites, whether LL.D.'s or honorific class offices, or the tactics and strategy of Operation Cornerstone guided by maxims in David's notebook?

# 13 / Town and Gown

*What the hell are cops doing on the field? I've never seen
cops on the field before. They ought to be at the university
where they belong.*

—MANAGER RALPH HOUK
in *Ball Four*,
by Jim Bouton

One time during the fourteenth century, the hostility between the townspeople of Oxford and the black-gowned students had grown sharper than usual. The carousing, wenching,
pilfering, and snobbery of the young men seemed no longer
bearable. Without warning, the townies attacked them with
bow and arrow, sword, and pike. The slaughter was much worse
than at Kent State. Probably the greatest provocation was the
same one that exasperates the population most today—puzzle-
ment about the content and purpose of college and university
studies, and resentment that the young people do not seem to
appreciate their privilege as students. Since only about one-
third of those who matriculated ever earned a medieval degree, compared with nearly three-quarters today, the frivolity

must have been greater then than now, and the population's resentment that much keener.

On the other hand, students have been charged with energy that could be triggered sometimes into violent explosion against the world off campus. The Yale students of the last century killed a fireman in one of their frequent bitter fights with New Haven functionaries. The memory of those events may still survive in town. It could explain the overreaction of the police to their snowballing by Yale students one winter not very long ago.

The society's animus against colleges and universities—the Town against the Gown—is perverse but understandable. It has created and supported them at great expense. One of its most basic, simple, urgent purposes in this enterprise has been to ensure a reliable following. Religious sects of the last century founded most American colleges in hopes of turning out young people who would keep the proper faith. In this century, government, industry, and the professions have maintained higher education expecting it to turn out useful man power.

But what happens? A college is founded, and students are gathered with enough intellectual bent to be able to sit still for several years over books, papers, and gear in classrooms, laboratories, and lecture halls. A faculty is assembled with enough culture and flair to give them academic stimulus. Students and faculty then become engaged with ideas, and some of these are abhorrent to the sponsors who made the dialogue possible. Is it any surprise that the college's sponsors and the nervous government and population to which they are responsible should demand that students and faculty be threatened with censure or discipline, or even be pummeled with night sticks?

Respectable medieval England knew it needed Oxford to breed churchmen and to tend to the theology that could ensure everyone's salvation. Englishmen could accept the strange notion that the scholar's occupation was constant argument. Some laymen even had an inkling of what they were arguing about, for instance, Tertullian's thesis that one's faith in a dogma should vary inversely with its credibility—the more absurd the idea, the more theologically reassuring. *"Credo quia absurdum."* It sounded complicated enough to be important. But then the suspicion would creep into lay minds that these arrogant academicians might be tampering with the sanctities. The most suspicious were the neighbors who saw other sides of university life. They had to pass a students' residence where the voice of one of them declaiming his disputation for tomorrow competed with the voice of a prostitute stridently arguing with another over her fee.

How much should the Oxford townspeople be blamed for now and then wanting to take arms against this mystifying, threatening, and often annoying elite? And how much should we blame a member of New York City's Tactical Police Force who admits he delights in beating college students? Why will the policeman then hold his victims down while two or three of his colleagues continue the beating? Why will he even blackjack to her knees a coed who is running away from him? And why will the nation watch all this on television, some of us with acquiescence, if not enthusiasm? And is there any real difference in the more formal harassment of our campuses by sheriffs through drug raids or by legislators through requiring discriminatory loyalty oaths from faculty?

Perhaps it is because we want higher education, and we do not want it. Some want the social mobility, some the class protection both of which this complex system provides. Some, like our medieval forebears, want salvation—this time not from Satan but from Communists. Behind those ivied walls masterminds are imagined hatching the scientific ideas with which we can head off incoming missiles. But what if they are not committed enough to heading off hostile foreign ideas? Worse, what if they are actually harboring them? Millions of Americans believe they are, like the parent in Plainfield, Iowa, who pointed out to a newspaper reporter that among all the dangers of sending his son off to college the worst was the chance that there "he might get to know a professor."

Insecure among their books, too many college professors do condescend toward anybody who is out in the world trying to get things done. Businessmen have been complaining that increasing numbers of college graduates, prejudiced by this campus condescension, refuse to go to work for their corporations. Many faculty even patronize their own colleagues, like those in the Engineering or Social Work schools, who teach the application of an academic discipline. And many condemn as mere popularizers those who try to share their scholarly ideas by writing and speaking to the public. Not understanding these men of thought, then, small wonder that from time to time men of action strike back at them. The fear of wrong ideas inside can infect all parties outside our campuses. Thomas Jefferson himself, "Apostle of Liberty," could not go all the way in his notion of academic freedom for the University of Virginia. "Now, about the appointment of faculty, Mr. Jefferson: Will their religious and political views be a consideration?" "Absolutely not. There will be perfect academic freedom." "Even Federalists may be appointed?" "Ah, well, now, our students will be young and vulnerable enough to require *some* protection. No Federalists."

The campus animus against the society—the Gown against the Town—is just as regrettable and understandable. On the students' part it is less perverse. After all, their studies have usually been from 200 to 2,000 years behind the times and by the most tolerant estimate today two decades behind. Condemning our science education, Einstein charged that a student who comes through it with any curiosity left has performed a miracle. Wouldn't young people naturally feel some pique toward the world that subjects them to such exercises?

In earlier times, American college students used to act out their frustrations against targets on campus. Frequently they burned the college's privies, and when these were rebuilt of brick, they blew them up with gunpowder. Occasionally, they aimed at more important college buildings. Someone set fire to the cupola of Princeton's Nassau Hall, and when President Ashbel Greene rushed out and saw the flames, he cried out that it must have been set by some young deist, a disciple of Jefferson or Thomas Paine. He was probably right, the arson being a protest less against the college's tyrannical regime than against the materialist ethos of early Federal America. Sensitive young spirits were already complaining that most of their elders had gone mad over money and property.

Student violence aimed more directly at the world off campus in recent times. One of the worst cases was the battle at the University of Michigan near the turn of the century. A traveling circus came to Ann Arbor, and some action of its crew provoked the students. During a long melee, they burned the tent and smashed much of the equipment.

Berserker destruction by students, often of local movie theaters or restaurants, has been occurring all through this century. In the early 1930's, I saw all the paddy wagons of the Cambridge precincts backed up in turn to a Harvard Square movie house. For no obvious reason that I can recall, a mob of undergraduates had wrecked the interior and were being arrested by the score. And after the vandalism by student revolutionaries at Columbia in 1968, the college daily printed a letter from an alumnus. He advised those who felt outraged by the damage to President Kirk's office that they should have seen the Nemo Theatre whenever the boys got through tearing it up in the good old days.

What was the source of this violence, beyond sheer high spirits and a yen for excitement and action? Perhaps it was their resentment of an unnatural segregation into a cadre to be trained to do the society's most difficult work. I recall the days at Haverford College when the boys would put in a fire alarm late at night. The volunteers of the local company tumbled out and roared up the hill in their trucks to be greeted by a crowd of students delivering a "locomotive" for them and singing college songs. Wasn't this to some extent the young men's defiance of the respectable, orderly society that some day they must direct?

Students sense that they are being disciplined and trained to rule. Rule whom? A grand view from the cliffs of Morningside Heights stretches to the East River—and a student inspecting it can see Harlem below him, blanketed with smog. Is this one of the populations they are being groomed to rule? Are the police and the hard hats two other such populations? The ferocity of the clubbings some students have suffered from them may express the resentment of those two groups as they anticipate their future subordination to the students.

The harassment of the last two national administrations by students and faculty has expressed anger over the Asian War. It may also have ventilated the old resentment of the Gown for the Town. Lyndon B. Johnson's government risked frequent exposures to it. He let his Secretary of Defense be mobbed at Harvard, his Secretary of State heckled at Stanford, his Secretary of Agriculture laughed off the platform at Wisconsin. He ventured onto the Princeton campus, where a large number of students and some faculty walked out on him. The war, of course. But more than that: the world. It's a great threat. And in our time, a Cabinet officer or a President is an extraordinary symbolic threat to an academic community— and a convenient target for retaliation.

In February, 1970, a group including a number of Columbia students struck in both directions. After trashing the offices of our Southern Asian Institute, they broke the front windows of one of the branches of the Chemical Bank of New York. At the college gate they engaged in a short scuffle with ten or fifteen city policemen who had come to intervene. On my way home from work, I happened on the university's Director for Student Interests disconsolately gazing at the footprints made in the lawn near the gate by the crowd of onlookers. He said he was stumped by this outbreak. Of course it was over the action in Laos, in particular. But it was so irrational. They'd made no prior attempt to get much support, no follow-up of any kind. It's more than Laos, more than the Institute and the bank. It's the role of young people the students are protesting. It's the larger meaning of their education. It's a protest against the society's manipulating them for its own vast purposes. Town and Gown? I asked. Yes, Town and Gown—on a continental scale.

The next action on the part of the Town in the old vendetta is expected by some to be repressive. A young alumnus teaching school on the West Coast just told me he sees an escalation of the antiyouth campaign out there, and he assumes one is building up in the East.

As long as young people are exposed in college to studies of the greatness of man while their own energy and spirit are underused, as long as their elders remain fearful of the desires for change these studies may arouse, no peace will be made between Town and Gown.

# 14 / Bust

*A young professor of French literature dropped in one day to chat under my maple tree. We found ourselves talking about education. What did he think was its purpose? He looked at me in astonishment. He'd never thought about that. Do his colleagues ever discuss it? No. Has his campus been disturbed by student protest? He cast a despairing look up into the leaves and sighed. "Let's talk about Montaigne."*

In the 1950's, the Columbia faculty apologized twice for the education it was offering. In 1957, the university-wide McMahon Committee called the American university, including Columbia, "a momentous institutional failure." Its report was a handsome blue paperback book of stately prose and careful data. It confessed to rigidity and narrowness in both administrators and faculty. Then in 1960 came the Buchler Report, made by a committee composed mainly of Columbia College professors. They exposed the undergraduate academic program. Out of date, inflexible, it was protected by the complacency and indifference of its faculty, "smothering in their own piety." If it were not reformed, someone would take the consequences, perhaps within a decade.

In eight years the whole university took the consequences of the inertia revealed in both reports. But the administrators bore the brunt. For their Bourbonism was more conspicuous than the faculty's, who gratefully joined in the condemnation of it. Only after the students had stormed the administrators' bastion did they begin to see that the faculty must be dislodged from an even more formidable position.

Nineteen sixty-six. Warmth comes into being. This was an organization that in one year was to involve over 700 students. At the start, led by one enthusiast, they had gotten from the university a large attic room, which they painted in psychedelic colors. Cold? Lonely? Come to Warmth and rap. They served food—free. They held a be-in in the park, a sweep-in in Harlem, and a sleep-in in our main quadrangle. They asked the college community for things—anything—which they gave away to people—anybody. They put on a Light Show. Near the Pupin Physics Laboratory, home of the first atom smasher, they started a tiny farm. According to the college paper, it included a chicken.

The *East Village Other* discovered Warmth and printed an article about it:

These Columbia kids could give hippies lessons in grooving on goodness itself, with neither paranoia nor pharmacological encouragement. It's quite a trip to find Columbia University's Warmth Committee—a little community of light and goodness right in the Center of the Power Complex—unmolested. . . . Warmth's idea of a loving community is identical to the underground's ideal of the tribal box. But somehow Warmth gets away with it, in spades.

The leader graduated, and Warmth disbanded. It was to reassemble a year and a half later, in the forcible occupation of some Columbia buildings.

Nineteen sixty-seven. Wasn't there a news report in the fall that the Students for a Democratic Society had chosen a half dozen universities to attack and cripple that year? And wasn't Columbia one? In their despair over the rigidity of the power complex, they would strike at its most vulnerable part.

So far, the student protest at Columbia had seemed more

theater than revolution. Here the setting is spectacular—the grand vista across the plaza and up the forty-five wide steps to the imperial façade of Low Memorial Library. This building houses the central administrators. It looms over the statue of Alma Mater. At her feet actors from our School of the Arts improvised skits satirizing the Fat Cats of the Society. Below, dramatically mounting the Sundial, an SDS leader would stoke up a mob of his brothers, then march them up the steps, brandishing a page of nonnegotiable demands, to find and confront the President. The drama might be heightened by the figure of a dean backing up and expostulating ahead of him.

April, 1968. Lovely weather. My secretary said she'd heard that there was some sort of trouble. Trouble? Yes, the students were occupying a building. Occupying it? Why? She didn't know.

They hadn't seemed inclined to violence. At a demonstration that stopped the ROTC commissioning ceremony some pacifists had broken a glass door. But in a panty raid on neighboring Barnard College, the first wave of raiders crossing the street had paused till the traffic light turned green. If they've occupied university buildings, at worst the police will drag them out, as at Berkeley's Sproul Hall.

"They've taken another one," my secretary said; this time she thought it was Low Library. This sounded more like war than theater. It reminded me of the words that flew around in the Easter Rebellion in Dublin: "They've taken the Post Office." Then word came that the architecture students had captured their own building. The *architecture* students? They're supposed to *build* them! Earlier in the year the teaching had been so bad in one of their courses, according to *Spectator*, that the class had boycotted it. But they weren't protesting their own school's numerous-enough drawbacks now, one of them said, so much as the inertia of the university.

The rebels' specific demands were first, cancellation of all military work by Columbia for the Institute for Defense Analysis; second, abandonment of plans for a gymnasium that would encroach on a park used by the black community; third, more democratic procedure in all disciplining of students; and lastly, amnesty for those students accused of breaking university rules in their protests.

To block the entrances to the buildings masses of desks, filing cabinets, and other heavy furniture had been hauled and piled into barricades. According to the *Spectator* staff in *Up Against the Ivy Wall*, their history of the crisis, the architecture students "had built critical stress points that would withstand the onslaught of hordes of police but would yield in seconds if altered in a particular way from the inside." Faces appeared at windows. A few sat on ledges and gazed amiably back at on-lookers.

Altogether, in the end, the number of insurgent students exceeded the number who had supported Warmth. But many seemed to be drawn from the same constituency. Their spirit, their style, were the same. We were able to talk with some of them. One sophomore was occupying the Mathematics build-ing. It was great in there, he said: everybody communicated, everybody shared, and everybody worked. His building hap-pened to have a stronger group spirit than the others—except the blacks, who had assumed control in Hamilton Hall. He wore a red arm band. That meant a certain revolutionary stance. Green, yellow, and black meant others. White meant concerned faculty; blue, students opposed to the revolt. Every-one had gained two great educational benefits that students tend to miss in a large university—warmth and identity.

The campus soon became crowded with the curious and the concerned. Here and there a pair argued and a knot gathered to listen, sometimes three or four deep. Many of us were very puzzled over what the university could do. Grant all their de-mands? Grant some? Grant none and call the police to clear them out? Leave the rebels in the buildings and go on using the rest of the plant? Close the whole place down for the re-maining three weeks of the semester? In hopes of hearing a convincing argument about one of these notions, we moved from knot to knot, the way they say men do in the streets of a Polish town. A social-work student and a law student, sur-rounded by a large and attentive crowd, were holding forth in a Homeric debate. The sun shone; classes had stopped; faculty

and administrators came out of their caves; we fraternized
with colleagues and others whom we might not have seen for a
year or so; a number of students chatted easily with professors
for the first time.

I stood beside a middle-aged lady. She spoke to me in a
German accent. She felt so sorry for us academic people in a
situation like this. We were so unprepared. "May I say, so
innocent?" She loved us for our devotion to ideas, to the mind.
But ruthless people will trample over us. We exchanged a long
look, and she turned away.

Just off the main campus large numbers of city police waited
in buses. Many of them were there for several days. Some of
those with high-school-age children were deeply puzzled. They'd
been saving money for their children's college education. They'd
moved to Long Island so that the school preparation would be
better. They'd even dreamed of Mike and Kathleen as students at a famous college. Here were other peoples' children
closing one down. A patrolman would go up to an undergraduate and soberly ask, "What's this all about, Mac?"

The university administrators decided early to ask the city
police to clear out the occupied buildings. One squad, led by
our precinct captain, eagerly started to, but some faculty stood
in its way, and the police began to knock them around. When
the administrators saw a professor's blood, they called it off.

Why did bookish scholars obstruct rampant policemen?
They believed that they could still persuade their students to
listen to them. In the end, why couldn't they? Because the
students perceived that the university had not been listening
to anybody. The Report of the Committee on Student Life,
though the result of two years' work by a blue-ribbon group
that urged only moderate reforms, had lain on the President's
desk for eight months, ignored. And the faculty had been
matching his haughty style in their own way, since it freed
them for more scholarship. The black students in Hamilton
Hall were even deafer to persuasion, mistrusting not only administration, faculty, and white students, but all white society.
Who had ever listened to blacks?

The burgeoning humanity and responsibility of our students

had met the resistance of an academic system that was well described by one of them the other day as "catatonic." Webster defines catatonia as "a stupor, often alternating with phases of excitement and marked muscular rigidity, and often accompanied with stereotypy of posture or activity."

An invasion from Harlem was threatened in support of the barricaded black students. One day, Charles 37X Kenyatta and his militants made a sally through the campus. A quick-witted dean, Henry Coleman, opened a path for them through a crowd of angry white students. The next day, an uproar began on the other side of the campus. "Here they come again," exclaimed nervous whites. Thirty or forty young teen-age blacks were imitating Kenyatta. Again, an alert white rushed ahead to clear the way. They stopped at the Sundial to make passionate speeches to each other through a bull horn, like Kenyatta. Both invasions had been symbolic, effective.

Wearied by suspense, a crowd gathered when three fraternity men came to the sundial, one dressed as an Indian in a loincloth, feathers, and war paint. Another introduced him as the Chief, who had something important to say. White man unfair to red man. Red man ask for even break. White man answer with forked tongue. Red man now make demands, positively nonnegotiable: one, return Manhattan Island to Indians; two, reissue buffalo nickel; three, rehabilitate Geronimo; four, provide free firewater for everybody. As news photographers snapped away, the Chief began to develop these themes. Fortunately, he was drunk enough to last only about five minutes. His brothers finally led him off, supporting him between them as they wavered toward one of the dorms.

A large group of faculty had gathered at an impromptu headquarters. Wives and secretaries came to do the telephoning and serve food. The men passed days and nights in negotiation, discussion, and vigil. Their first purpose was to persuade the students or the administrators or both to give ground. Neither did. But it was the faculty's influence that delayed for a week the decision to clear the buildings.

A second purpose of some faculty was to stand peacefully but firmly in the way of anyone using force, including the police.

They would accept the injuries that might result either as the cost of their failure to negotiate a settlement or as an atonement for years of general faculty neglect of students. A young professor of engineering described these two sentiments a few hours before the major police action. The next day I heard he was in the hospital with three broken ribs.

Even more than police intervention, the faculty dreaded violence between students. Hundreds of angry ones had formed the "Majority Coalition," as they called themselves, determined to thwart the rebels. A few clashed in small fist fights. A mass battle seemed likely. The Coalition was gathering to assault an occupied building. As several professors tried to dissuade them, one student got a ground-floor window open. At this desperately critical point, Professor Robert Belknap, of the Russian department, climbed up to a ledge. Tall, lean, still wearing his fur hat against the cold of the April weather, he began to talk quietly. They were soon straining to hear him.

They all took Humanities A, he reminded them, the course he directed. So they knew that since the Egyptians, the most constant and difficult problem of man has been the balance between liberty and authority. Even Saint Augustine, whose *Confessions* they read, had his troubles with it in his youth. Of course, direct application of liberal education to real life, Belknap admitted, is so rare that most of them probably hadn't ever been asked to do it. But why not now? Several of the hottest places in hell, according to Dante's *Inferno*, are reserved for people who can't see that reason is superior to passion and force. Soon after the professor had finished, the crowd dispersed, sending representatives to meet with the faculty to discuss a compromise. Before long Belknap was appointed Dean of Students.

The compromise consisted of an agreement by the Majority Coalition, most of whom were athletes, to use no force except in a nonviolent siege of the occupied part of Low Library, the psychological center of the strike. They would let no person in. They would let no supplies in. But they would take no other initiative. Just in case, the faculty formed a cordon, too, between the students of the Coalition and the building, in whose windows the exuberant or defiant or sometimes derisive faces of strikers could be seen. Their supporters outside soon began to come near enough to heave supplies over the heads of both the professors and students into the second-floor windows. One by one, a quantity of potatoes would be rapidly fired into outstretched hands, followed more slowly by a dozen loaves of bread and then still more slowly by two-quart cans of juice.

When the campus crisis first began, some nervous administrators accused the college radio station of aggravating tensions through sensational on-the-spot reporting. In fact, our nerves were steadied by WKCR's generally accurate information. It flowed from transistor radios in peoples' hands all over campus. This reduced movement and cooled emotion. What's happening over there? Someone speaking through a bull horn or shouts or a squad of police filing into position. Instead of hurrying to see along with hundreds of other excited people, we found a nearby transistor and heard WKCR's description of the event, probably more complete than the perception of it by many bystanders. Later, the New York *Times* radio editor praised this student reporting as more responsible and effective than most professional radio and TV coverage of crises in the world off campus.

All gates had been closed but two, and faculty were admitting only persons with university identification cards. In quick succession to one gate came these three. First, a senior professor who demanded to know by what authority anyone could stop him at the gate of his own university. The checkers waved him in and begged him to look around and see. Second, a big, steely-eyed man, who brushed past without showing identification or even acknowledging he'd heard the request for it. The checkers asked a nearby police captain if he knew the man. Yes, he was a plain-clothes commander. Then please persuade him to say so; we have a hard enough time. "Mister, the police are here for only one purpose: when the time comes, to break heads." Third, a short, slim, dark-haired, youngish man with a strong, sensitive face. His ID card, not a university one, read Thomas Hayden. A checker showed the card to his colleague. Isn't he the radical leader? Yes. Let him in; they need seasoned people in those buildings.

Under Hayden's influence the occupants of the Mathematics building experienced participatory democracy at its best. It was used in all the occupied buildings, but his personality inspired a special sense of responsibility. Problems were aired and all decisions made by wholly unconstrained discussion and the vote —how to get the garbage cleaned up or whether or not to resist the police. Hundreds of the strikers still cherish the memory of getting things done, from housekeeping to high politics, by means of unstructured discipline.

In Fayerweather Hall, without an unusual leader, the same method led to rambling talkathons. This building was populated by the least revolutionary group. With a high proportion of graduate students, it was gentler and not so political. Here the "liberated life" was lived even more generously than elsewhere. Here one morning someone had stolen around and left an orange by each person. But as the days went by, the most moderate in Fayerweather grew politically sophisticated, especially through measuring and responding in their own way to the tough, doctrinaire leadership of the central strike leaders.

I've been surprised by the hostility toward those leaders expressed by some strikers. "We despised them," one told me who had negotiated with them several times. Their task was to squelch the inclination toward compromise, which lay close to the surface in the rebel population. Their task was to keep the genuinely revolutionary feelings of the mass of strikers focused sharply against the university administration until the police came.

Some months before, I had heard Mark Rudd deliver one Sundial speech. He was forceful and amusing. "So we'll screw those cats up there," he shouted, pointing to Low. "As a matter of fact, they're all screwed up anyway. You can see they've been screwy enough from the start. And the trouble with them probably is they just don't know how to screw." The University Proctor, who should have looked stern under such circumstances, was laughing. To his appeal as a speaker, Rudd added persistence and some ruthlessness. He depended not on the native democracy used in the buildings but on concentrated Leninist oligarchy.

Throughout the revolt, a sizable minority of the students were playing little part in it. They may have been detached observers of one or two of its incidents. Suzy predicted it might tie up the university for some time, took a bus back to Cleveland, did the leg work to line up a summer job, and followed the Morningside Heights ordeal in the *Plain Dealer*. Herman redoubled his efforts to finish a major paper on Arab-Israeli relations, since the library of the School of International Affairs stayed open and there were few users to compete with. A number alternated revolution and normalcy, like Chris: he rushed out of one occupied building to play in a tennis match with the Navy and then rushed back in.

Steve studied and loafed in his room, went downtown to a movie, ate a Chinese meal at the Moon Palace, stopped in to talk with friends, and occasionally went to a place on the roof of the highest dormitory, which offered a panorama of most of our troubled campus. From there, in the very early morning he watched as the occupied buildings were emptied and the police commanders, like Roman generals after a long siege, allowed their men to act out with their night sticks and blackjacks some of their resentment. One of my sons, a news photographer for the New York *Post*, was there. The paper put on the front page his picture of a student cornered by a policeman who was raising his blackjack as high as he could reach. In token of total disillusionment, the college newspaper the next day left its editorial space blank.

In his history of Harvard, Samuel Eliot Morison described an especially violent riot in the 1830's. President Josiah Quincy called in the constables to stop it, many were arrested, and trials were held outside Cambridge. Morison asserts that his action lost Quincy any rightful control over the students and aggravated campus tensions for years to come. The police intervention at Columbia reached a savagery that surprised everyone but the blacks, most of whom knew policemen at their worst. But unlike Morison's early students, large numbers of ours were turned by it more against the society than against the university. The rebellious students were expressing concern over the death of Vietnamese and Americans in Asia and the life of blacks in Harlem and of young whites on campus. Parents, alumni, and the press expressed concern mainly over an interrupted academic schedule, over damage to buildings and furniture, and over the cigars and sherry in the office of President Kirk. "And can you believe it—they actually drank up the President's sherry."

The faculty engaged Professor Archibald Cox of the Harvard Law School to determine the "underlying causes" of the uprising. His Commission invited anyone with relevant information to testify at hearings. Perhaps to ensure a friendly verdict, his Commission was heavily weighted with faculty from other universities: another law professor, a sociology professor, a university psychiatrist, were balanced by a solitary layman— a judge. They invited anyone with relevant information to testify at hearings. These were held in the McMillin Theatre, where the commissioners sat on the stage behind a large table covered by a green baize cloth. Witnesses spoke into a microphone at a desk on the floor in front of the stage, and a court stenographer took down all their words.

In general, the Cox Commission's appointment by the faculty was overlooked. Instead, it was mistaken for an effort by the administration to defend and clear itself. One young man whom I would call representative of a large number of the university's students got up from the front row to leave one of the hearings. He saw me in the back of the theater and made a long detour around most of the house. He leaned over, whispered hello, pointed to Chairman Cox, looked at me as though I had invited this eminent lawyer and law professor, and hissed, "He's a pig." I was astonished to hear a relatively moderate student so describe a person I perceived as warm and fair. Seeing my reaction, Arthur leaned over again and added, "He's a *smooth* pig." He gave me one more indignant look and then stalked off toward a distant side exit.

Naturally, the parade of witnesses during several weeks of testimony had included almost none of the insurgents. A few other students and a number of faculty turned out to put the blame on the university's administrators and trustees. Under this partisan barrage the Commission kept its head. Its report, *Crisis at Columbia*, summed up the turbid event and its causes with clarity and objectivity. Also, it was pervaded by a quality lacking in almost all the parties directly involved: humility. *Crisis at Columbia* distributed the blame widely. The administration had been much too conservative and unresponsive to students. For years, the faculty had left virtually all important decisions and action to the administrators and put students a very poor second to their own research and writing. The students should not have used force. Agitators from outside Columbia were relatively unimportant.

The balanced realism of the whole report was too much for the New York *Times*, the Columbia *Spectator*, and the university's trustees. The students should not have used violence— but they had to. That is the conclusion I read in *Crisis at Columbia*. The *Times* took it as a condemnation of violence. The *Spectator* complained that the Commission had "come down on both sides of the fence." I have it on good authority that a number of Columbia trustees condemned Chairman Archibald Cox as a pinko.

But greatly to its credit, the Commission faced the issue once raised by the Buchler Report: that something is dangerously wrong with the curriculum of higher education. They concluded that it is overly vocational and technical. Wisdom is ignored. They quoted a long passage from J. D. Salinger's *Franny and Zooey* in which Franny recalls that in four years of college only one professor ever used the word "wise." A political scientist applied it to Bernard Baruch, whom Franny described as "some nice old poopy elder statesman who'd made a fortune in the stock market."

In the years since the revolution, many students and younger instructors have come around to the view that the underlying causes of America's campus disturbances are mainly educational. The academic inertia of the professors has built up deep frustrations in the students over many years. Their anxiety over current social and political crises aggravates these. The autocracy of the administration sets off the explosion.

# 15 / Presidents

*It wouldn't take a high wind to carry this college off. A heavy rain would do it.*

—JAMES H. CASE
President of Bard College, mid-1950's

"The American college president is the most universal faker and variegated prevaricator that has yet appeared in the civilized world." In 1921, Upton Sinclair wrote those words in *Goose-Step*, a book exposing the exploitation of professors. Big business dominated them more arrogantly than today through boards of directors interlocking with boards of trustees. Professors were humble but resentful. The person who tried to reconcile the factions was the college president. He had to reassure both the men of action outside and the men of thought inside. In one role he must appear to command, in the other to conciliate. But Sinclair recognized the difficulty of this task and in the end condoned the duplicity of college presidents. He insisted they *had* to be hypocrites.

Today, even though the interlocking has become less tight, presidents are still squeezed between the world and the campus. In fact, the squeeze may be even worse because of the youth revolt. For students tolerate compromise less easily than their elders. A certain president seemed to me to be struggling hard at reconciling various groups of impatient partisans. "He's a flaming liar," exclaimed an undergraduate. But I think that deep down the young man forgives. I can count six presidents of institutions in the Northeast confidently branded by many of their students as being alcoholics. My guess is that this is a tribute. The students are really saying that it's an impossible job.

The central process of administration is decision making. The best administrator gets others to make the most decisions. A college president more than any other sort of executive must excel at this delicate statesmanship: send up a trial balloon at a faculty meeting, put a flea in the ear of the student president, play devil's advocate to the trustees and Prince Charming to the cleaning ladies. But sometimes he must take things in hand like a Napoleon: a heroin ring has just been discovered in a dorm, the alumni in a Southern city refuse to sponsor the debaters' visit because they have just competed at a black college, the history department hasn't got a chairman because neither of the senior professors can stand seeing the other chosen.

College presidents have called themselves a lightning rod, a punching bag, a beggar, a schizoid, a Man of Sorrows. One has a recurring dream. He's standing in the center of a crossroads. Toward him, down each of the four roads, charge herds of buffalo. All are equidistant from the intersection. And he can't move.

Today a few university presidents must take on a more heroic responsibility: the launching of essential academic change. Faculty, free as scholars but hidebound as professionals, have always resisted substantial improvement of their curriculum and teaching. Students, with the freshness of youth but the futility of inexperience, are good academic critics but poor innovators. Trustees, alumni, parents, are out of it. Only presidents, like the navigator of a ship, are in a position to see a new and better direction and change course. But they will do this only if they are academically farsighted. Rarely have such men headed our colleges and universities.

America found several in the decade or so after the 1860's, the Creative Period of our higher education. They could see ahead, and they could move academic mountains. Called out by a crisis, the collapse of the classical Renaissance curriculum, they were as adroit, practical, and tireless as our best presidents today. In addition, they were educational evangelists. Their gospel was the scientific method. They brought about the only major reform in the history of American higher education.

How were these men found? How did members of the Harvard corporation in the 1860's see the promise in Charles W. Eliot, a shy, young MIT chemistry instructor? The right side of his face was disfigured by a large liver-colored birthmark. He was not much of a scholar, and the educational ideas he brought to his presidency were offensive to a large proportion of the men on the university's governing boards. Yet he was to shape their institution into the first great American university. He did it by liberating the undergraduates, through the elective system, from the strait jacket of required studies; he did it by building graduate departments; he did it by opening the way for modern studies, especially science. His administrative style combined patience and decisiveness. As the new president, he attended every committee meeting on the university calendar, carefully noting the least quibble. He plunged into every student riot like an avenging angel. Picture him at one of the bonfires in the Harvard Yard, fueled with college property, by which the boys used to express their alienation. Over there a student struggles to heave in another mattress. Who's that tugging at the opposite end? Why, it's young President Eliot!

In the 1870's, what guesswork led that successful but unsophisticated industrialist, Ezra Cornell, to appoint as his first president Andrew Dickson White? This young man had already been director of a bank, a railroad, and a canal. He had served as a diplomat abroad and as a state senator in New York. But he had also taught history at the University of Michigan under President Henry Tappan, another early crusader for high scholarship. Over the years, White had dreamed, talked, and planned a more democratic education than the classical curriculum provided. Against fierce opposition from educators and powerful laymen, he made Cornell a university where not only upstart subjects like physics and French but farming and forestry were offered together with the classical studies. In books and speeches, some published by the first official university press, White also helped convince the nation that modern science does not exclude religion. After three years, Cornell enrolled a larger freshman class than any other American college ever had.

What wisdom inspired the founders of Johns Hopkins to turn to Daniel Coit Gilman? He had already gotten into trouble as president at Berkeley, an institution even then harassed by politicians. The Hopkins trustees, against the advice of three of the country's most eminent presidents, asked Gilman to make theirs a university mainly for graduate study. He packed his faculty with brilliant investigators into exotic or dangerous subjects like philology, evolution, and sociology. With no student activities nor campus, the institution is said to have been mistaken by some townspeople for a piano factory. Among the first students were young men of the caliber of John Dewey, Frederick Jackson Turner, and Woodrow Wilson. Johns Hopkins soon reached the scholarly stature of the German universities and set a standard for America to follow.

The choosing of college presidents is considered a mystery. Out of three centuries of experience and a little recent research, modern trustees say they have drawn no clear guidelines. Their three other principal duties—raising money for the institution, protecting it from outside attack, and taking very general responsibility for the quality of its education—seem like relatively simple ones compared with their fourth duty: presidential search.

How can our trustees today pick another group of great progressives? Looking back, we can see three conspicuous and probably crucial factors in the success of these pioneering presidents: first, they all entered office with clear and passionately held ideas about new academic subject matter; second, they had already proven their unusual administrative skill; third, they were so young, none commencing beyond his thirties, that they could give not only creative but long service to their institutions. The shortest term was White's eighteen years at Cornell, the longest Eliot's thirty-five at Harvard. The group total adds up to eighty-two years of brilliant leadership. Eliot, the most influential, suggested the value for reform in long presidencies: "I outlived my major opponents on the faculty."

An inspired leader can again overcome the inertia of the American university. In our century only one Prometheus has emerged with all the qualifications of those earlier reformers. He is Robert Maynard Hutchins, President of the University of Chicago from 1929 to 1951. Can we find others like him? In case wider familiarity with his presidency could make that easier, here is my version of the story of Hutchins at Chicago.

When Hutchins was first appointed, he was not quite thirty. From his previous position as the "Boy Dean" of the Yale Law School, he brought knowledge of how to get things done against heavy odds. Yale was taking a giant step away from training young men for corporate law or ambulance chasing and toward educating them for broad and deep legal thinking. In advancing an old law school in that direction, Hutchins had learned how carefully the quarterback, when facing a strong defensive line, must decide whether to call a center rush, an end run, or a time out. An old Eli tells me Hutchins refreshed himself down at Mory's playing clarinet in jam sessions with Rudy Vallee. He already had a distinctive educational philosophy. It was romantic, but it was coherent; and he flaunted it like an oriflamme. David Riesman heard him captivate a luncheon audience of Chicago businessmen by the excitement of his defiance of their values. "What we want at the university," he declared, "is more red ink in the budget and more Reds on the faculty!"

Karsh of Ottawa soon photographed President Hutchins for *Vanity Fair*, bringing out both his dash and his depth. The magazine showed the picture in a series including those un-beatable pitchers the Dean brothers. Dizzy Dean, with the most graceful delivery and the fastest ball in the majors, and Bob Hutchins, another champion stylist, were dazzling the National League batters and the Chicago academicians. I met one of Hutchins's young professors in a French railway carriage during the summer of 1936. After our discussion of the ex-citement at Chicago, we found we'd ignored the beauty of Burgundy and even missed the statue of Vercingetorix on that hilltop near Dijon.

Under Hutchins, Chicago was developing the most dis-tinctive academic program ever offered in an American uni-versity. Crusading for intellectual excellence, he declared that collegiate education should focus wholly on the mind. Its goal should be the grasp of principles, of those eternal factors that pervade the passing flux. The academic way to that end is the study of the liberal arts. He clinched these propositions with a syllogism worthy of his beloved Aristotle: "Education implies teaching. Teaching implies knowledge. Knowledge is truth. The truth is everywhere the same. Hence education should be every-where the same."

Together with some colleagues, Hutchins confidently boiled the heritage all down to the Synopticon, a selection of 100 books. These contain the essential ideas. To teach the ideas at the university, new courses were clustered under four topics—biology, physical sciences, social sciences, and humanities. This new pattern, which has since been copied almost everywhere, brought order into the chaos of the latter days of Eliot's elective system. It helped undergraduates see the similarities and the differences between the truth of a chemist and the truth of a poet.

Also, knowing that many professors either would be reluctant to teach in this program of general education or would sabotage it, Hutchins set up a separate faculty, drew top scholars to it, and gave them just as much backing and prestige as the rest. They turned out a steady flow of introductory textbooks, which set a new standard of readability and authority. They threw themselves into helping a group of bright young intellectuals cultivate their intellects with the relish of Ionian philosophers. They joined Hutchins in condemning the fraternity frivolity, vocational preparation, and varsity athletics, which distract young people from the life of the mind.

Those students with keen scholastic appetites ate up the new Chicago fare. A chemistry teacher at an upstate high school reminisced the other day about Hutchins's image to students in the 1940's. "He was very handsome. And he was funny. And he was shocking. We adored him." He shocked educators by admitting qualified candidates who had finished only their sophomore year of high school. He shocked them by sweeping away the system of academic credits to be accumulated like poker chips: when his students could show in exams that they knew their subjects, they advanced. He shocked them by awarding the B.A. degree for as few as two years of work to those who could prove they'd earned it. He shocked laymen in that heyday of big-time athletics, especially Chicago alumni who had played for Amos Alonzo Stagg, by discontinuing varsity football. And to make the most of America's delight in self-flagellation, he shocked the whole country with several books blasting the mediocrity and utiliarianism throughout U.S. higher education. He thundered against them in the tone of one of the angrier Hebrew prophets, though with some unprophetic sparkle.

Hutchins was blitzing American higher education very much the way young Peter Abelard had blitzed the school of Notre Dame in the twelfth century. Revolutionary, electric, each simplified the complicated—Abelard a theology, Hutchins an academic culture. They clarified the loose, the aimless; they challenged the smug. Abelard risked excommunication, if not the stake; Hutchins risked jeopardizing a great university.

In fact, Hutchins's reforms brought difficulties with the benefits. I met a few stragglers from the Hutchins crusade in the early 1950's. After a year of it, Severn Darden, the actor, wanted to transfer to an earthier or a more whimsical campus. The Chicago Dean told us that Severn had been reported wearing a cloak and sword, even to his classes. Daniel Newman, the painter, said he couldn't stand all the arguing. "It's like law school," Danny complained. "And don't ever mention the name of Aristotle to me again." I was told by college advisers of high schools in the Midwest that the only students the university attracted any more were those we would now call "freaks." In an article in *The New Yorker* about the city of Chicago, A. J. Liebling described the undergraduates of the college as the "greatest collection of juvenile neurotics since the Children's Crusade."

Furthermore, the academic world boycotted the two-year degrees, though the only objective evidence I've seen suggests these undergraduates were in at least as good psychological and academic shape as any other bright American college students. Also, affluent donors began to regard as a group of dangerous radicals the independent thinkers Hutchins eagerly attracted to his faculty and harbored there. These donors were giving their money elsewhere. Finally, to many people Hutchins's denunciation of our educational system began to seem extravagant. To some his history seemed wrong. He alleged that his call for more emphasis on the mind and on liberal rather than vocational studies was in the true tradition of Greek and medieval education. It wasn't. Greek educators did not concentrate on the mind until, through political failure, they had nothing else to concentrate on, and then they trained it mainly for professional uses. The medieval universities were overwhelmingly dominated by theology, law, and medicine. What liberal arts studies they offered were downstaged by the specialists.

But education will respond to a leader who may be impractical or even wrong if he's stylish, plucky, productive, and bold in his ideas. In 1951, Hutchins was inveigled into retiring to take other high positions of cultural leadership. The university began a slow reaction back toward normalcy. The campaign for attracting junior prodigies subsided, the freshmen were given booklets containing all their photographs to re-create class spirit, a Dean proclaimed that once again "brawn would be respected along with brains," the university's leaders stopped harping on unorthodoxy, and the graduate school specialists resumed their sway. Stagg Field, where the Maroon had once battled the Wolverines and the Badgers, saw students playing football again, though now against Hiram and Beloit.

But the best effects of Hutchins's Chicago Plan remain. His philosophical spirit lives on. The Chicago fans root for the team with Aristophanic irony. "Kill! Kill!" they shout, as their backfield gets in motion against a line of equally scholarly middleweights. In a recent season, they fielded between the halves a band including a cello and a fifteen-foot kazoo. Academically they can buck the fashionable stampede toward relevance by entering an experimental department, the New Collegiate Division, which offers a modernized approach to the "classical and Christian heritage." Or they can major in philosophical psychology, a reaction against today's mania for study of white rats and perceptual stimulus-response patterns.

The Chicago professional schools, too, are more speculative than most. A Business School professor laughed when I asked if he used the case method of instruction. "Much too empirical for us," he bantered. A Medical School professor interviewing candidates for admission apologetically assured them that his colleagues do, after all, teach their students to take out an appendix. The Dean of the Library School warns that he wants to turn out not librarians but thinkers who will dream up the library of the future. It will contain no books. To help design it, he will gladly admit to his school, among others, engineers with a taste for new ideas.

And some of Hutchins's unusual concern for teaching survives at Chicago. Excellence in it is still recognized by several awards to faculty, whose salaries rank third highest among the country's universities. One of Chicago's ace teachers, biology professor Joseph Schwab, published a book in 1969 on how to do it—*The College Curriculum and Student Protest*. There he describes "The Chicago Approach." It is the method of Socrates. It requires a fatherly, genial, tireless instruction in the analysis of "fundamentals"—a Hutchins password. And the highest form of teaching goes on in the faculty dining room, where round tables draw together scholars from different disciplines. They emulate Alfred North Whitehead: when asked how he developed his mathematical ideas, he replied, "I dined."

Altogether, the University of Chicago is supreme in a quality that I can only call "class." I believe it is the special gift of Hutchins. In *Where the Girls Are*, Peter Sandman and his fellow authors select the girls at Chicago for the only unqualified praise they give:

A vibrant island of very active people in the midst of a surly, life-less Chicago slum, the College breeds exciting women. The Chicago girl is bound to have very strong interests (arts, drama, and usually liberal political causes), and if you're on her wave-length, she's quite likely to get very excited about *you*. You may find the Chicago lass taking notes in the darkened balcony at an Albee play or telling her boyfriend about her roommate (or her roommate about her boyfriend) with copious references to Jung and Adler. Chicago is a unique college, hard to joke about. Cosmopolitan and enlightened, its student body reflects nothing more than the personality of its ex-chancellor, Robert Maynard Hutchins.

One reason why Hutchins succeeded so brilliantly was the nation's need for him. After a war, a boom, and a crash, America of the mid-1930's craved leaders of strong voice, bold character, and fresh thought. But the spread of his influence was limited because of the excessive intellectualism with which he justified some very progessive reforms. Aristotle and Aquinas were models of creativity, and their achievement was finding new solutions to new problems. But Hutchins borrowed only their solutions. He tried to keep us in the straight line of the syllogism. Reliance on abstract discussion of justice by the old logic, as in the study of Plato's *Republic*, does not appear to prepare people well enough for the realization of justice in the world around them. For that, more nonlinear education would help, more attention to the "field" of the syllogism, more concern about its relationships and applications to life. Hutchins was not radical enough. Nor were the country's educators ready for the radical thinking required to meet the challenge of this great academic insurgent.

After another war, a boom, and a slump we need presidents like Hutchins. Can our trustees pick such men again? Why not? Only two or three universities, involving a few dozen trustees, may lead the way. And on each of the two or three boards only a few imaginative, aggressive members are needed to discern a gifted reformer and persuade their colleagues to appoint him. Fortunately, trustees are almost all laymen rather than educators and therefore more capable of choosing a person with unorthodox ideas.

Historian Walter Metzger, in his book *Academic Freedom in the Age of the University,* assures us that trustees tend to be neither good nor bad but to vary in the quality of their action directly with the quality of the presidents they choose. In the 1890's a time of white-hot antilabor emotion, the Regents of the University of Wisconsin were asked by the Superintendent of Public Instruction to fire a prolabor economist. Some Neanderthals like Ed Keller of Thurber's *The Male Animal* may have been among them. In the play, Ed commanded the Dean, "Get the reds, get the reds; and when they're all gone, get the pinks." The Board was certainly packed with conservative men of affairs hostile to unions. But their president was Charles Kendall Adams, a distinguished scholar and powerful administrator. Under his influence they refused to fire the vulnerable young economist and explained their decision to the people of the state in a report ending with these words:

Whatever may be the limitations which trammel inquiry elsewhere, we believe the great State University of Wisconsin should ever encourage that continual and fearless sifting and winnowing by which alone the truth can be found.

Even a C. K. Adams could not save a great university today. It needs more than fine administrators. It needs seminal thinkers. The American nation has begun to perceive the obsolescence of its higher education. Like our ancestors in the 1860's and 1870's we are becoming disillusioned with it. Our colleges and universities must undertake another grand design for a radical reform of subject matter and teaching. Our attention must be directed from crises to ideas. The crisis managers in fashion these days for college presidencies can only prolong our ordeal. Only academic thinkers can lead us into a new academic age.

# 16 / John Dewey

*Perfection means perfecting, fulfillment fulfilling, and the good is now or never.* —JOHN DEWEY

In 1970, the Post Office Department put John Dewey's portrait on the thirty-cent stamp. To many people his name means nothing. Others may be reminded of a Spanish-American War admiral or a New York State Republican governor. Still others will remember Dewey as an educator. "He brought on all this permissiveness."

Dewey began writing in the 1880's. In *The School and the Society* (1899) he urged that education admit its age-old vocational function and try to perform it better. *Democracy and Education* (1916) is a masterly argument for learning in which students take more initiative. *Human Nature and Conduct* (1922) is a work of social psychology that Dewey's bitterest critics call a great book. It explores the tension between man's need for change and his urge to resist it. The disastrous consequences if we ever succeeded in resisting it is the theme of *Quest for Certainty* (1929). Fortunately, he promises there that the quest will always be in vain. At the age of eighty, Dewey published his last major work, *Logic: The Theory of Inquiry* (1938), already a classic of post-Aristotelian thought. In it, as in all his works, he argues that we should judge ideas by their results.

A generation ago, a good deal of talk was heard about Dewey, but few people read his books. We happened then to need a scapegoat to punish. Word got around that this influential Columbia professor was subverting our ancient values of discipline and scholarship and his followers were ruining our schools and colleges. So if we did not ignore him, we either ridiculed this hardheaded Vermonter as one of the impractical progressives or denounced him—then America's only great living philosopher—as a menace to the nation.

Dewey used the term "student-centered classroom." He meant by it nearly the opposite of the selfishness it has often implied. Start with a young person's own interests, he urged, because his best enthusiasm arises out of them. Then lead him on, enthusiasm and all, to discover the "funded wisdom of the race." He will then grasp and hold to that more firmly because he came to it more on his own.

Certain experimental colleges of the 1930's followed this principle. They required freshmen to choose and focus all their energy on some keen present interest of their own. One would start with the poems of Baudelaire, another with Kepler's laws of planetary motion. But each would encounter problems whose solution could only be found elsewhere. Why were the French poets so very eccentric? Why did one of them lead a lobster down the street on a leash? Read the history of middle-class France under Napoleon III, and see what they were reacting against. How could Kepler believe that angels rode the planets? Read Plato and Dante to understand how deeply the European mind imbued the world with spirit.

A student wants some philosophy? First ask him about his own. Is it pessimism? Positivism? Hedonism? Mysticism? So he's a logician? Then have him try Wittgenstein's symbolic logic after some study of the symbols he's using himself: "trip," "freak-out," "generation gap," "ecology," "cool." He will probably be shocked by and interested in the ambiguity they mask. He will understand his need for expert help to use them responsibly. Then he'll want Wittgenstein.

Donald Tewksbury, who presided over Bard College nearly forty years ago, illustrated this Deweyan principle by the metaphor of a tree. Narrow at the bottom—but firm—each student's education broadens into a wide reach of branches and foliage as he discovers that he must explore more and more varied subjects in order to understand his original one. A poetry major might turn up in a physics class in his senior year in order to know more about form, while an astronomer might demand instruction in psychology to discover why astrology has such a following. The Bard Plan of the 1930's, based on Dewey's ideas, was designed not only to allow but to encourage this evolutionary growth.

The concept of "student-centered education" was mistaken by many people to mean impulsive and aimless self-indulgence. And too often, attempts to apply it led to chaos in the classroom. The phrase could serve as a slogan rather than as a challenge to imaginative action. It signaled progressivism to the extent that wearing an American flag in one's lapel signals patriotism.

Another concept important to Dewey was expressed in the phrase "educating the whole man." He hoped to lead educators away from teaching a young person in sections—his intellect today, his conscience tomorrow; the first in the classroom, the second in the chapel. Few college faculty offer science as social and aesthetic instruction. That's for other departments, they say defensively. The laws, data, and laboratory method are absorbing enough. But science can also teach internationalism, humility, love of beauty and mystery. And the simplest scientific fact has a spiritual dimension. What is more awesome than Galileo's law of inertia: a body, undeflected by another force, will move at a uniform speed, in a straight line, forever? "Forever" is a solemn word. The physics professor may know more about it than the chaplain.

Dewey was arguing for interdisciplinary study to educate a total person. At the colleges that attempted to apply his ideas earlier this century, the faculty of various departments were encouraged to work together, teaching with their disciplines combined. A course on the Middle Ages might involve a group of students in simultaneous study, say, of the economics, medicine, and theology of that period.

I first heard of Dewey from my father, who taught summer school at Columbia in 1913. He often lunched at Dewey's table in a small restaurant near campus. He recalled scientists and engineers hobnobbing there with humanists and philosophers as though they were an Academy of Amateurs from the Renaissance.

Dewey also believed a total education must involve much art. Although he considered scientific intelligence applied throughout life to be the only hope for civilization, he gave more support to the creative arts in the college curriculum than to the academic sciences. He believed that in the studio more creative intelligence is used and more meaning developed than in the laboratory as it is set up today.

"The artistic personality is a mixture of spontaneity and intellect," wrote the late Stefan Hirsch, Professor of Art at Bard College. A Bard faculty survey of the pattern of courses taken showed that those majoring in creative art chose a greater number and variety outside their own field than did science, social-studies, or literature majors. And at Bard it seemed also that the artists' initiative and originality inspired the others. The example of a student putting his whole self into his art encouraged his friends to do likewise in their traditionally more superficial, narrow, and imitative academic study. In addition to their usual work as majors in physics, economics, and biology, Pete made a discovery in the conductivity of metals useful to a nearby manufacturer, Doris scooped the professional economists with her research into decentralized merchandising, Joel bred the first pure strain of wild mice to be used in cancer research.

John Dewey tried to practice what he preached. Did he make art as well as write about it? I don't know. But he was a good judge of it, according to one artist. At an auction at the Parke-Bernet Galleries in New York City, he noticed an elderly man up front who he thought must be a dealer, for he bid only on the best pieces and aggressively only on the very best. Who is he? the artist asked. That's Professor Dewey from Columbia, an attendent replied.

When the phrases "student-centered curriculum" and "educating the whole man" came into use thirty or forty years ago, you'd have thought they were obscenities. Many academic people still throw a fit if you use them. They fear the challenge to the academic tradition that these express. One college professor hawked loudly when I mentioned the name of Dewey and spat as far as he could downwind.

Dewey upset the academic world worst of all by his insistence that study should be related to action. "Learning by doing" was the phrase coined to convey this thought. People who acquire their knowledge as a detached exercise always tend to keep their ideas and their work separate and remain irresponsible in one, unimaginative in the other. Before World War One, Dewey was calling for more relevance in education. He did not use the word as a slogan. His main concern was its definition and application.

In the 1930's, some progressive colleges took a step toward greater relevance by trying to hire for their faculty a few non-academic men and women. An articulate and thoughtful businessman or industrial-research scientist might bring fresh meaning to economics and chemistry, which would have gone unperceived by a lifelong academic scholar. A fine idea. But few such persons were found and hired.

Alternate work and study, the co-operative-college movement, has been so successful that even Dewey's worst enemies must concede a victory for learning by doing. Work-study programs such as those at Northeastern University and Drexel Institute of Technology were once counted in the dozens but are now counted in the hundreds. Northeastern has been introducing them into graduate fields such as business, mathematics, and anthropology, and most recently into its new Law School.

John Dewey was capable of vigorous action himself. According to a former Bennington professor, he may have saved that college at a trustees' meeting in the early 1930's. He was a member of the board, which had failed to raise enough money to open the institution. The wealthy board members were inclined to give up. Dewey assured them that if they could not raise the funds, he and his progressive friends would.

Ironically, Dewey believed that his ideas had been applied best in certain Russian schools. In the 1920's, progressive education was the method officially and dogmatically required, in the Russian manner, throughout that troubled nation. When Dewey visited the Russians during those years, he was received like a hero. Unfortunately, most of their education system was even less ready to respond to the progressive methods than our own. Even worse, the party planted loyal youngsters in classrooms to see to it that they were excessively "student-centered." The aim was to demoralize the teachers, who appeared to be a serious obstacle to the acceptance of Communism.

At home, an alleged deterioration in our moral fiber was traced by many critics to the permissiveness they said Dewey's ideas had propagated. In 1938, Dewey wrote *Experience and Education,* in which he pointed out that American schools and colleges had not yet applied his ideas widely enough to have done any harm—or good.

Today those ideas are alive again, usually without credit to Dewey and probably often without knowledge that they were tried before. In some experimental colleges, like Fordham's Bensalem, a beginning student can pick out one topic of keen interest to him and devote his whole time to it, hopefully branching out later, like Tewksbury's tree. Interdisciplinary teaching is being tried at some lively colleges of only moderate prestige—Centre College of Kentucky, the University of Houston, and Southwestern at Memphis. At Southwestern, professors of physics, visual arts, religion, communication, and music have teamed up in freshman colloquia. The relating of study to real life and work is escalating in the co-operative-college movement. Elsewhere, the earlier exposure of graduate students in medicine and law to clinical work and legal action is being matched in gingerly exposure of undergraduates to the world out there. Even traditional Columbia offers an "Institute," in which an upperclassman works for an entire semester of credit in a political-science project requiring much outside, nonacademic experience.

Is this a favorable sign? Are we for the first time to give Dewey's ideas a good trial? He is the modern Aristotle. He provides us with the philosophy for the next development in education. Aristotle's has been a steadying hand. But our mounting troubles are a sign that we need another hand, one that knows how not only to rein us in but to let us go, and one that can help us toward better knowledge of our whole selves.

John Dewey gathered up the strands of reform that had separately interested various reformers for 500 years. Some denounced pure mental training in the early Renaissance when the Athenians' interest in both the mind and the body was rediscovered in ancient classical literature. A few educators succeeded in offering a more rounded education in several brief experiments, like Vittorino's school for the Marquis of Mantua. Again, some seventeenth-century educators criticized the detachment of learning from the objects and processes it is all about. Then, too, a few pioneers briefly introduced the real world into their classrooms, like the Czech John Comenius, who put illustrations into schoolbooks. In America, mideighteenth-century progressives deplored the insulation of higher education from direct vocational teaching. An abortive attempt, supported, by Benjamin Franklin, was made at the University of Pennsylvania to introduce practical studies and value them as equal to the classics. But this impertinence had been squelched by the early nineteenth century and up to now has been fought off successfully. Lastly, after the American Revolution, in planning the University of Virginia, Thomas Jefferson proposed that the students discipline themselves. His impulsive young Southern patricians couldn't or wouldn't. Then a number of colleges, beginning in the 1930's, tried again. Antioch, true to its century-old tradition of progressivism, even put students on committees that decide on admitting other students and on hiring and dismissing faculty. Neither did this movement spread widely into other colleges, except as condescending tokenism.

The massively inert academic system stifles small, brave attempts to rejuvenate it. It resembles the medieval university in its later days, so inhuman and so narrowly professional that it was an easy target for the satirical fire of a Renaissance writer like Rabelais. He contrasted to it the education of his hero, Gargantua, who was offered not only academic learning and athletics, but politics, crafts, travel, gastronomy, and good manners: "more like the recreation of a king than the study of a scholar."

Dewey insisted that we must lose our fear of the Gargantua in us: he is our source of drive and should be educated rather than suppressed. A modern Gargantuan education will enlarge the concept of vocation to include our life as well as our work. It will teach young people to understand the future as well as the past, the unknown as well as the known, failure as well as success, death as well as life. Above all, it should teach them to regard change not as a threat but as a way of life.

In 1941, I was granted an interview by John Dewey in his apartment on Central Park West, New York City. I recall an Edwardian decor in browns and a kindly sage with snow-white hair, very dark eyes, and the face of one who has understood and accepted the ironies of life. A slight misalignment of his rimless spectacles suggested the absent-minded professor. I asked this Nestor why his ideas have been so resolutely ignored by educators. It takes time, he reassured me. Maybe they haven't been presented well enough. Surely another generation will be ready for them. He looked hopefully at me, then all of twenty-nine years old.

I recalled the dictum by which Dewey tried to reassure impatient prophets, in *Intelligence in the Modern World:*

Let us admit the case of the conservative: once we start thinking, no one can guarantee where we shall come out, except that many objects, ends, and institutions are doomed. Every thinker puts some portion of an apparently stable world in peril, and no one can wholly predict what will emerge in its place.

# 17 / Careers

*"These, these are all my accomplishments," he said, a note
of defiant pride steadying the quaver in his voice.*
*"These, these were your efforts to resist me," replied Death,
and took him in an unguarded moment between projects.*

—LOUIS J. CANTONI
in "No Time to Die"

How much difference does formal education make in a
person's competence at work? Professor Ivar Berg, of the
Columbia Business School, decided to find out. He surveyed
people in several organizations. Were the more effective ones
those with the most academic preparation? They weren't. He
then examined other careful studies of the same question. They
too showed no substantial correlation between degrees and
effectiveness on the job. In the spring of 1970, he published
his findings in a book, *Education and Jobs: The Great Training Robbery.*

Dr. Berg is a sociologist. Tall, deep-voiced, he lectures in an
educated New York accent on the realities behind the for-

malities of American society. I heard him discuss with a Business School class the rituals with which educators disarm their constituency. Take commencement, he proposed. Parents have been kept from the campus for four years. They've been unsure about the value of all those rather impractical studies. They've felt uneasy over the return on their costly investment in them. Now at last they become reassured by the sonorous commencement address, the notables humbly coming up for honorary degrees, the academic procession, the mayonnaise stains from ceremonial chicken salad at commencement luncheon. Mom and Pop can go home with the notion that their thousands of hard-earned dollars were well spent.

A student in the class objected here that for hiring and promotion employers demand the degree he will get at commencement. Isn't the employers' belief in it important, justified or not? Yes, it's important "for vocational placement in a society of buttondown personalities and gray-flannel mouths competing to breathe the technicians' polluted air."

After finishing *The Great Training Robbery,* Professor Berg was promoted to the position of Associate Dean of Faculties, where he probably will write no more embarrassing books.

*The Great Training Robbery* should embarrass nearly everyone. A large proportion of students attend and then stay in college because they think it's necessary preparation for a job as good as their father's, or better. Parents contribute money mainly for the same reason. Faculty profess a loftier purpose: Education develops you, many a catalogue promises, so you know not merely how to make a living but how to live. But then the faculty offer studies heavily slanted toward professional scholarship. And since President Eisenhower, the leaders of the country, often through advertisements in buses and subways and magazines, have been urging upon the young a college education as a necessity for a respectable job.

So Dr. Berg's warning may be needed. Not by everyone, though. Thousands of high school students hesitate over going to college in the first place. Thousands who do go, bored or even hostile over what they find there, are asking about alternatives to further study or to corporate jobs. They've begun to suspect the entire formal education system. And thousands of their elders agree. Graduate study is coming in for especially sharp criticism from those it should help. Many newspapermen declare any journalism school a waste of time. Business education is now under heavy fire from business men. Social workers are accused by their clients of being prepared mainly to perpetuate poverty. For years all sorts have indignantly been condemning graduate study in education and work for the Ph.D. as obstacles to the preparation of good teachers. Doctors admit that a large proportion of what they studied in medical school is of no use to them in practice. And two years ago a federal judge became so unhappy with our young lawyers that he resigned from the bench to head the Notre Dame Law School and send all his students to England for their second year of study.

On a different basis from Dr. Berg, another embarrassing freethinker has challenged the parade through the four-year college and its extension through the indeterminate uplands of the graduate school. Professor Seymour Harris, a Harvard economist, prophesied twenty years ago that just about now a surplus of college graduates would begin to glut the job market—and would continue to for an indefinite period of time. His calculation was simple: take the inordinately increased number who would be coming out of college; put it over the normal growth of the job market; subtract. The difference would be a proletariat of many thousands of degree holders with no appropriate jobs.

I remember Harris from the early 1930's, a friendly young tutor attached to my House at Harvard. As a classicist I then looked down on all economists, even such an engaging one. Fifteen years later he didn't ingratiate me further with his dismal prediction in *Market for College Graduates and Related Aspects of Education and Income,* nor later still when I heard him repeat it in the mid-1950's in a speech to an admissions conference. Nor did he prevail on his fellow man-power economists. Up to now, most of them have argued that the more bodies a society draws into its higher-education system, the greater its economic strength. They did prove that college graduates' lifetime incomes average double those of high school graduates. But the economists did not prove that the college-going is a cause of the national productivity or of the individual wealth. It could be an effect. Or it could be unrelated.

Seymour Harris's first warning came shortly after World War Two. But you can't respond to every siren. At that time other louder ones were frightening us over our trained-man-power scarcity and our seemingly infinite backlog of need for goods and services. Harris was dismissed as a crank or else ignored. During most of two subsequent decades of intoxicating capital expansion, when employers grabbed at any personable college graduate with convenient credentials, Harris was forgotten. Then the Johnson Administration froze federal hiring in 1967; the reason given, our exorbitant military budget. A little later several corporations warned us that they could hire very few of our graduates that year; the reason given, a campaign against duplication and underwork. More recently still, when employers throughout the country cut their hiring drastically, the reason given was the Recession.

But some of us fear that a deeper reason for all this bearishness in the job market could be Harris's factor: the over-all supply of college-educated young people passing the over-all demand. It may bring a deflation of the occupational value of higher education.

For several years such a deflation has been foreshadowed by some employers inclining away from job candidates with the doctor's degree and even the master's. Right now they need to pay the lowest salaries they can. But even before the Recession they were telling us that a person with a bachelor's degree often contributed better work in a shorter time. How long does it take to get a man with a Ph.D. to fit in and produce? "About eight years," answered the research director of a chemical company. His counterpart at an oil company said a good man with a B.S. can do useful, creative work in a couple of years, under skillful supervision. "And they're less likely to try to run the firm."

Then, in the summer of 1970, the Department of Labor announced an increasing need for technical specialists without a bachelor's degree. They need only some preparation in high school or in a post-high-school institute or in a two-year college. Today one technician works at drafting, calculating, measuring, tinkering, with every two or three graduate engineers. It should be the other way, say leaders in that field; two or three technicians working with every engineer; he to think, read, talk, scheme, they to help him put his conjury to work.

Human relations is another field in which less-than-collegiate preparation may become increasingly valuable. This field is expected to boom. It will need a greater range of experts. Not far from Columbia I have visited an institution called GROW —Group Research, On-going Workshops. With no academic affiliation but with state accreditation, GROW offers a certificate for extensive training in over a dozen methods of group leadership. It prepares paraprofessionals, the word describing a person with formal training up to the level of the engineering technician or the GROW graduate. GROW should turn out persons like one paraprofessional who does not have a high school diploma. In his forties he was a tugboat captain. Now he offers strong and sensitive behavioral analysis and guidance. He is a successful man-power consultant. He told me of attending, a couple of years ago, the first annual conference of the American Society for Humanistic Psychology. The word "paraprofessional" sounds more attractive all the time. It smacks of a freedom from the priestly rigidity of the professional.

Further academic deflation can be seen in the growth of studies without academic credit taught where people work. Read about it in two books, *The Classrooms in the Factories* and *The Classrooms in the Stores*, by Professor Harold Clark, of the Columbia Teachers College Economics Department. In these studies he reports a vast amount of formal post-high-school education offered within industry. Surprisingly much of it includes study of the liberal arts, which some corporations have been offering in-house, on company time, at nominal cost. This is a return to the conditions of apprenticeship. In early America an employer had to promise to the state, and bind himself to the promise on an indentured bond, that he would teach his apprentices not only to work at his craft but also to read, write, and behave. With few schools for them to attend, this was a good enough substitute. Many employers undoubtedly were a far better educational influence than the tobacco-chewing derelicts who taught in many schoolhouses. Today's trend described by Dr. Clark suggests a similar solution to the staggering problem of financing our colleges and universities and modernizing their academic programs: substitute more education by employers.

Of course, the sense of deflation of academic and occupational values is keenest among students. Several candidates for law school who could have gone to the best ones asked their advisers this year for information about the worst. They want to learn only enough to pass a bar exam somewhere, hang out their shingle, and become a sort of Atticus Finch, the genial, sensitive, small-town lawyer in *To Kill a Mockingbird*. Raised, like them, in privileged families, two other seniors came in to talk about how to become a policeman and a cook. One had seen police mishandle friends too often over drugs. The other had done the family cooking after his mother's death and loved it. Neither career requires further academic study, though college-level training is available for the ambitious.

Do all these signs—Berg's exposé, Harris's prediction, paraprofessionalism, off-campus study, and the alternative career—point to the decline, if not the fall, of our system of higher education? "Tear it down!" the campus revolutionary commands. Should we at least let it collapse—gently?

Curious about the opinion of a seasoned economist of education, I put in a call to Professor Harris. He has retired from the Littauer Professorship of Political Economy at Harvard and sequestered himself in autumnal peace on the faculty of San Diego State. He remembered me from the 1930's. "Come on out," he begged. "It's wonderful!" Yes, the job crunch looks like his prediction coming true. Yes, he sees the college-educated proletariat beginning to emerge. No, it won't be a disaster to higher education, necessarily. Could be a blessing, in fact. "Remember my cheerful closing prophecy in that speech at the admissions conference?"

Like most of the conferees, I suspect, I had been too shortsighted to take in the importance of Harris's speech, let alone remember how he ended it. Maybe we suppressed our sense of its importance out of anxiety. As I scanned his speech in the booklet of the College Board Colloquium of 1956, I noticed Dr. Harris's warnings that the first sign of an unemployment crisis for college grads would be a surplus of teachers. He was right on that; the Labor Department announced it a year ago. But what was the good cheer he spoke of on the phone? It was at the very end. Only one sentence: "If the economic case for higher education comes to count for less with time, the need to stress its larger values will become doubly vital."

What "larger values"? Will its vocationalism give way to humanism? Does Dr. Harris think that the American college, as it becomes less economically practical, can be made more educationally satisfying? Does he hope that this institution, founded by Calvinists and enlarged by specialists, can be matured by humanists? Can American higher education become less a credentials service and more a school of the mind and spirit?

# 18 / Placement

*"What are you going to do now?"*

*"What am I going to do now? There isn't much choice. I can
stew in the East. I can rot in the Middle West. I can freak on
the Coast."*

"What do they do to you in here?" Several years ago a newly
arrived freshman poked his beanied head around the doorway
into our career-advising office and asked his sophomore guide
that anxious question. The word "career" threatened him, as it
does many other young people. It suggests, first, a routine you
get locked into. Second, it suggests, as he said, what somebody
else does to you. The freshman feared if he so much as stepped
inside our door, someone might zap him, like David Balfour
when jealous old Uncle Ebenezer tried to have him shanghaied
off to the Carolinas. We career advisers lie in wait to lure you
into the race for the trillion-dollar gross national product and
the Pax Americana. We're doing secretly what General Hershey
did openly in the draft and called "channeling."

Not that we don't try to correct this image of our office. When I was appointed to it in 1964, a new director had just persuaded Central Administration to change our name from "Office of University Placement" to "Office of University Placement and Career Planning." He hoped the new word "career" would convey our interest in helping people fulfill themselves. It did not. Instead, it conveyed the impression that we are not only trying to help people fit into slots, we are trying to program their whole lives. Our director then guessed the misunderstanding might lie in that word "planning." So he tried again; he got permission once more to change "Career Planning" to "Career Services." Great, we thought, it sounds less manipulative, more supportive.

But students remained suspicious, perhaps seeing themselves being channeled even more insidiously. Their suspicion of us is understandable in part because of our office's most visible role: the arranging of visits by recruiters from industry, government, the professions, the military. Since the faculty and a large majority of our students recommend "open recruiting," we'll schedule interviews for any organization a number of them want to explore. The only "organization" I recall we've ever rejected was described by its undergraduate backers as the National Liberation Front. "Did you say the—ah . . ." "That's right," they interrupted, "the Vietcong." We were damned then for saying no, just as we've been mobbed and even smashed up for saying yes to recruiters regarded as serving our own warmongers.

Students may also suspect us because we touch too important a part of them. Even with the much heralded but still relatively rare four-day week, a person spends more of his time in his life's work than in any other one activity but sleep. He may well be diffident about discussing with strangers a matter at once so fateful and so personal. Men in four Massachusetts colleges revealed this diffidence to psychologists who were studying attitudes toward work. The conclusions of the study were published in a chapter of Nevitt Sanford's book *The American College*. To these young men, work is as deep a concern as love. Both are too deep to discuss even with a close friend or a roommate. They feel doubts about their competence: Will I be a good lover? Will I be a good worker? Those questions are too intimate. At twenty, it is difficult to discuss them with anyone, certainly not with some functionary in a career office who appears to represent the industrial barons.

Still, more students do overcome their fears and venture into our office these days, usually first into the Career Information Library. Those who've gotten it all together barge in confidently. That senior over there with a pile of company literature on his table is finding out about jobs in the food industry. He'll try to get into the marketing division of a large firm. After learning the ropes, he may transfer to public nutrition work in developing countries. And that young woman with *Peterson's Guide to Graduate Education* wants to be a politician and is checking out professional preparation, like Rutgers' Eagleton Institute of Politics or the Fels Institute of Local and State Government at the University of Pennsylvania. She's in no doubt about her career—her job last summer in the DA's office clinched that.

And it isn't the New York City phone book in the hands of the insurgent over there with shoulder-length hair. It's the U.S. Labor Department's *Occupational Outlook Handbook*, the best compendium on work. He's after information about printing. He will learn a skill needed in the Movement. This was the object of one of his fellows we saw haunting our library for a couple of weeks. We'd seen him before only at a mass meeting, where he got the microphone right after the President of the university and the Mayor of New York City and called them pigs.

But our library is used by other students who have been only pretending they've picked an occupation. They say, "It gets you off the hook," or "Now I can tell my friends something," or "I had to shut my parents up." By their artificial decision they've contrived a moratorium from self-examination. They may drop in to look at literature about law or teaching, choices that shove the real decision away for several years. The graduate preparation required allows them to shift to something else. This was its main value to one person who has just graduated from the Columbia Law School. Steve estimates 90 per cent of his class there entered in that halfhearted spirit. How many still feel that way? "Ninety per cent." Steve hotly defended this estimate. "We've been thrown together by our common ambiguity."

Our librarian describes another type who seems to drift in. She asks if she can help them. No, no, they protest, as if they might bolt. She sees them probe around a little and take down the catalogue of a foreign university, an IBM recruiting leaflet, the *Peace Corps Reader,* a directory of occupations for women, *Careers for Engineers. Vocations for Social Change, The Draft and You.*

Others don't come near our career-advising office because they're hanging loose about the whole bit. They have better things to do. Their career? They couldn't care less. Don't worry, for the present they'll get something to keep busy—and solvent. Even if you could show them their destiny, they wouldn't look—thank you very much.

These cavaliers are encouraged by some eminent vocational experts such as Professor Eli Ginzberg, Professor of Economics at our Business School, recently Chairman of the National Manpower Committee, and author of *Occupational Choice,* which triggered a new and more scientific wave of study of careers in the early 1950's. Dr. Ginzberg is small and frail-looking but sparkles in conversation and publishes important books almost annually. While we talked, his secretary popped in and out with messages and questions. Dr. Ginzberg gave me just one piece of advice about trying to guide the young in their careers: "Don't." Tell them to take all the math they can stomach and get good at one foreign language. Beyond that they've got to plunge in somewhere. Yes, but where? "Anywhere." He told me a nephew was coming down from Yale soon for vocational advice. He sighed apprehensively.

But some of those who follow such advice do come in to see us anyway for tactical help, if not strategy. It's usually shortly before or after commencement or during their first year out. The world has begun to appear a surprisingly tough place, even to achieve modest solvency. For that, they've been driving a taxi and have just been held up for the second time. They're to be married next month to a bewitching girl whose salary as a secretary for American Widget downtown already seems like the only sure income. All four parents want to help, but darned if you can surrender to *them*. Yet. Those career advisers should have some useful ideas about how to get bread. And they just might advise you how to get some without selling your soul to the barons.

Here comes one now, personable, urbane, but a little anxious. On our office form he's put *B* average, major in history, fraternity treasurer, football squad, disciplinary board. What can we do for you, Ron? Help me find a job. What sort of job? Any sort; I don't care too much—provided it's interesting and pays well. Have you heard of the Recession? Have I? I've been going the rounds for weeks. Why didn't you come in here before you graduated? I didn't really know of your office. Never even heard of it? Oh, I did hear the name, I guess, but you know. Yes, we know. Have a cigar (one out of three accept one).

I then asked Ron to think back over his whole life and recall something he's done with special pleasure and done well—by *his* standards. At any age, anywhere, for any purpose. "Something I enjoyed?" Ron is stupefied. Like millions in our middle class, no one's ever asked him to take seriously what he enjoys. Thought of anything yet? Yes, he has, but he says it's irrelevant. I remind him I haven't said anything about relevance. Only about something he's loved doing. Ron then tells me how in his freshman year of college he saw a young woman hit by a car. The victim lay under the front end, the driver stood by in hysterics, coeds were screaming from windows of a nearby dorm. Ron yelled for all the men in sight to come and lift, told a girl to phone for an ambulance, sent a boy racing for a policeman. You say you *enjoyed* this, Ron? Well, yes, the girl was in shock but conscious, and when they eased her out from under, she gave him a look he'll never forget.

Other persons using our method of functional self-analysis report "successes" such as these coming first to mind: making a fine Frisbee throw, building a model of the Globe Theatre, cleaning fish, leading the eighth-grade math class in the teacher's absence, walking in the rain, reconditioning a wrecked Austin-Healey, raising rare trees and shrubs, improving on jokes and anecdotes, putting out three runners at the plate in a close game, collecting the beer cans of all nations, placating a hostile cop, keeping a regular diary. One person with his older brother set fire to a curtain in their parents' absence—the brother ran, but he stayed and put it out. A young woman at the age of fifteen won a city-wide bubble-blowing contest in Pittsburgh. Another told me first of sand castles he used to build. But he wasn't just building castles, he was getting others to join him in the task. His main satisfaction came more from this teamwork than from the design or the construction. It satisfied him even more than the dike he always recommended so his team could continue on long after the tide had destroyed the work of others. He was the statesman of the beach. The George Washington. In a number of his later "successes" he found he had repeated this diplomatic, firm, prudent leadership.

The study of such experiences, both early and recent, helps our students discover a direction or change their present one or confirm it. It can then help them find an employer who needs what they have to give. One American firm with much business abroad faced growing problems in its foreign branches and needed a cosmopolitan trouble shooter. One of the vice-presidents saw the résumé of a recent graduate, written after a functional self-analysis of his whole past experience. John had vaguely decided on a business career. But where? What? How? He'd been ricocheting around personnel offices and agencies and answering ads in the paper for some time when he came in. He was very down. "I've worked hard for my college degree. I want to work hard for an employer. But none of them wants me." As unemployment accelerated, John slowed down and studied his experience carefully. One of his happiest memories was visiting foreign ports as a seaman on freighters during his summers off from college. What made him enjoy this so much? Exploring a new community, quickly mastering the locale, meeting the people, discovering the ethos. He was also proud of his good relations with fellow seamen. And he doted on maps. He'd also got a kick one college vacation learning fluent French in a Swiss summer school. What else? Buying a run-down sailboat in his early teens and overhauling it. Why did he recall that? Oh, you take something in disorder, put it in order, improve it, see it work. Enjoyed anything since graduating? No, he'd done nothing but get turned down a hundred times looking for work. Except one temporary job for a few months. But he'd hated that. Hated all of it? Matter of fact, one part of it, no. The job was as a U.S. census supervisor. The federal bureaucracy is ridiculous, but the directing of several dozen people was great. "Power I love." Anything else he's loved doing? Yes, there's another that seems silly to mention. Go ahead. Well, it was this: as a senior in high school in New York City, crashing dances at fashionable girls' schools. He refined this pastime to an art, if not a science. John then went off to write all this down, with details, and add other accomplishments he recalled because of the happiness they'd brought him. Then he discussed this material with us and analyzed it to see what functions or factors were operating most often when he was doing anything happily and effectively. He decided they pointed to foreign travel, problem solving, authority. He then put this aim down on paper and supported it by a list of his favorite experiences, arranged in order of importance to himself. You can read the document at the end of this chapter. What's more, the vice-president read it and offered John a position in international personnel: visit a foreign branch of the company—say, Tokyo—and get to know quickly the local culture and the adjustment to it of the company's people; report to New York your findings and suggestions for improvement; then move on to Hong Kong to case things there; then on to Jakarta, and so on.

John took a critical step in his job campaign when he needed to see an executive of this company who would not grant him an interview. John crashed.

This method of reporting your values was developed by Bernard Haldane, who directs the Bernard Haldane Seminars in Washington, D.C. It was introduced at Columbia by Saul Gruner, vice-president of Thinc Career Planning in New

York City, trained by Haldane. The other day I told Gruner of three of our young alumni who had just gotten jobs doing exactly what they wanted—John was one. Two of the employers were laying off managerial staff at the time. Even more intriguing, all our three got jobs made up for them according to their favorite experience as put in their résumés. How come? I asked Gruner. Easy, he replied. Remember the opening sentence of *A Tale of Two Cities*: "It was the best of times, it was the worst of times. . . ." Well, today seems like the worst of times in employment. Lots of qualified candidates, few jobs. But these are the best of times for job hunters like your three. Since employers are hiring so few, they'll examine applicants much more carefully, and they won't miss those who describe their experience so simply and helpfully.

Those sketches should help answer the question the freshman asked: "What do they do to you in here?" Our people come in with too little sense of their worth. That has been eroded in their formal education. They have accepted as their identity a College Board score, the name of a college, a set of grades, an academic major, a campus activity, a relatively hollow decision toward a graduate discipline, a law-school entrance-test percentile. We ask them to identify themselves at their happiest and proudest. When Eileen puts in her résumé "planning an entire Girl Scout camping weekend" and Bill "kicking a nine-year smoking habit," they are telling an employer about basic satisfactions and strengths most helpful to him in evaluating them.

Would an employer reading this book want to meet Donna? All of nineteen, she'd quit high school in a small western Massachusetts town and come to the East Village. In a year or so she was hooked on heroin. They sent her to me for discussion of her future. We discussed her past.

First, she wept a little and asked why people are taking the trouble to help her when she's no good. I said she'd see in a minute. Then she dried her eyes and recalled an early love of carnivals—an experience, she agreed, not unlike New York City. Next, she recalled the happiness of handling horses. A friend had owned a couple, and Donna enjoyed taking metic-

ulous care of them but also riding them at a gallop. She liked
being thrown and getting right back on. But her greatest satisfaction had been in gym during high school. Donna had won
state championships on the parallel bars, in tumbling, on flying
rings. The joy of it came from intense concentration on a skill,
from working and performing on her own, from winning out
in tough competition, and, above all, she insisted, from doing
something beautifully. "Beauty I love."

"Now, Donna," I said to this dejected young woman about
to undergo the trial of methadone treatment, "suppose I
described a person to you as follows: she has endless patience
in important tasks, great independence, unusual physical courage, and a high standard of excellence. She also works best
under pressure and seeks out risks. What would you say of
her?" She allowed herself a broad smile for the first time and
said, "Groovy."

Donna says only her great-grandfather still believes in her.
In his mid-eighties, he is retired from the police force of a
New England town but is now hard at work as a security
guard in a nearby college. Old sir, I'd love to know you.

---

John L. Parker
Room 306
Foreign Student Center
Columbia University
New York, N.Y. 10027

*Objective*
> A position that would make use of my extensive foreign travel,
> my educational background, and my managerial experience.

*Qualifications*
> * Successful in relating to a wide variety of classes and national-
>   ities of people.
> * Several visits to Europe, England, and Japan.
> * Direct managerial experience.
> * Speak fluent French.

*Educational Background*

Graduate of Columbia College, 1969.

Attended L'Ecole Lemania, Lausanne, Switzerland. Summer, 1968.

*Travel and Work Experience*

Three summers working on American freighters and one Norwegian freighter. Ports of call: West and East coasts of the United States, Panama Canal, Japan, British Columbia, Northern Africa, Spain, France, Italy, Yugoslavia, England, and Holland.

Summer, 1968: Used money saved from working on ships to live in Switzerland and study French. Traveled through Paris, Nice, Vienna, Frankfurt, Amsterdam, Brussels, London, Geneva, Zurich, Neuchâtel, Lausanne.

*Present Job Activity*

Supervisory Crew Leader with the U.S. Census Bureau. Responsible for 8 Crew Leaders and 45 Enumerators.

*Urban Interests*

Maps and their development.

Cities and their development in relation to their place and importance in history.

Explore urban resources to the fullest.

Wrote two major and successful papers on complex urban problems.

*Other*

Straight A student in math in high school. Took advanced-placement math and went directly into second-year calculus at Columbia.

In early teens overhauled, maintained, and raced my own sailboat.

Skipper on High School Varsity Sailing Team.

Strong side end on High School Varsity Football Team.

Member of Junior Varsity Heavyweight Crew Team at Columbia.

*Personal Data*

Age: 23; Height: 6' 2"; Weight: 185 lbs.; Single; Excellent health.

# 19 / Critics

*President Eliot (here he is again) used to say that so long as a strong spirit of pessimism prevailed in all departments, he knew the university was flourishing.*

One of our first acts after arriving in the American wilderness was to build schools and colleges. No sooner were they built than we began to complain about them. Maybe it was the cost, payable in scarce pennies and "pine tree" shillings, in wheat, wampum, and—as historian Samuel Eliot Morison imagines—"an occasional ill-favored cow." Or maybe it was just the poor quality of the education. Anyway, our ancestors went on complaining steadily, regardless of improvements in quality. The cost, of course, has been rising steadily for 300 years.

Both the schools and colleges have always been vulnerable to criticism. In the seventeenth century, President Increase Mather said he found the young men sent up to Harvard ineducable, and his son, Cotton Mather, attributed this weakness to a "Creolian degeneracy" in the lower schools. Many of the citizenry, once including Governor Henry Vane, were also very critical of Harvard. They thought it too intellectual. They ridiculed "the Black-coates at the Ninneversity." In the early eighteenth century, Harvard was still unpopular with many, this time for the opposite reason. Now it was not intellectual enough, by orthodox standards. The boys were accused of reading "plays, novels, empty and vicious poetry, and even Ovid's *Epistles*." In protest, the colonists founded Yale.

In the eighteenth century, schools were generally so bad, in many areas because taught by indentured servants, that the privileged often hired tutors or educated their children themselves. An advertisement in a Philadelphia paper read, "Lost: one silver watch, one sorrel horse, one schoolmaster." But the colleges also seemed unsatisfactory. Benjamin Franklin complained in his newspaper that the young men came out of them "as great Blockheads as they went in." What was worse, toward the end of the century our campuses became infested with the spirit of religious freedom preached by Thomas Paine in the *The Age of Reason*.

In the nineteenth century, while the Boston School Committee "blushed for shame" over the reading, writing, and spelling of their best pupils, critics kept on denouncing our colleges. An apprehensive low-brow like one Midwestern legislator would protest, "I was born in a briar thicket, rocked in a hog trough, and never had my genius cramped in the pestilential air of a college," and a scornful high-brow like Henry Adams would complain that the four years of college work could be done in four months.

In our century, the schools have consistently been dismissed as a mindless lock step. At the turn of the century, Thomas Edison insisted that our elementary education was a relic of past ages. "It consists of parrotlike repetition. It is a dull study of twenty-six hieroglyphs." Not long after that, Abraham Flexner began to thunder against our colleges for their superficiality, and against our universities, Chicago and Columbia especially, for their "bargain basement" curricula. Unlike most education critics, Dr. Flexner practiced what he preached, creating the Institute for Advanced Studies in Princeton, New Jersey, to show just what he meant higher education to be.

Over the centuries, the critics have usually concentrated on either our lower or our higher education as their target. They do not seem to have enough ammunition for a barrage covering both systems at once. Imagining, for instance, that the flight of Sputnik I was a triumph of Russian elementary and secondary education, they ignored our colleges and universities in order to belabor the schools for their weaknesses. Red tape in teacher certification, overemphasis on sports, "life adjustment" courses for unsophisticated youngsters, new and controversial reading methods for beginners, automatic promotion —critics pounced on such gropings and exercises, the growing pains of our school system. They held them up as signs that it is sick, if not dying.

For the duration of this blitzkrieg, college and university educators were safe. Just as vulnerable as their colleagues in the schools, they stood off and watched with relief, some even egging on the critics. But their turn came a few years later, after the students' hair grew long and their occupation of college buildings frequent. In the 1960's, the critics rediscovered the weaknesses of higher education: subversiveness, too little discrimination in admissions, faculty detachment, poor teaching, permissiveness. Those who had been roaring for the blood of educationists were now shouldered aside by others bellowing for the flesh of academicians.

Careful study of what lies behind our everlasting carping reveals a pleasant surprise—education is usually improving, but too slowly for the human eye to see.

Elementary and secondary education plods along. It progresses—but on an even and very slow course. It kept this pace all through the nineteenth and twentieth centuries, steady and undramatic. Daylight was substituted for gloom in the classroom, humanity for the whip; a start was made toward the substitution of thought for memory, ideas for facts. A college degree, rather than a few years of grade school, became the requirement for teachers. It was said that in Pennsylvania before the Civil War any man who could stay out of state prison would be welcome to teach school. By now, schoolteachers have not only forged a profession but also aspire to make it a respected one.

But these changes have been gradual—like the growth of an oak. They can be measured, then, only by comparison over a long stretch of time. And the gain has come too slowly for many to appreciate it as it came. While the critics' beat was prestissimo, the educators' tempo was adagio.

Our colleges, too, have been improving with the slow but irresistible speed of a glacier. They have been prodded along as a consequence of innovations like the Land-Grant Acts, the elective system, the strengthening of the natural and social sciences, graduate study, honor programs, the GI Bill. But critics of higher education, like the others, do not take a long view. Instead, they too concentrate on the system's current troubles and imagine that it is going downhill.

A popular complaint today, for example, is that professors are pulling away from their students. They aren't. Instead, the students want (or say they want) to be closer to their professors. So it's not the professors who give less but the students who want more.

Faculty of old were usually stern Calvinists to whom young people did not wish to be close. The Dartmouth professors of the early nineteenth century, writes a historian of that college, were each assigned to a section of the college and the village—where many of the students lived—"acting partly as spy, partly as inspiration to the good." At faculty meetings, when no obvious mischief remained to be punished, the President would read down the list of students, asking for information concerning their general "moral delinquency." To this supervision the response of the students in our typical colleges was an embargo on friendly relations with the faculty. A student who went to a professor's room unsolicited or who stayed after class to ask a question was guilty of "high crime."

The current charge that college professors do not take their teaching as seriously as of old is also unfair. Far more teaching, in any meaningful sense of the word, goes on in our classrooms now than during the last century when the faculty, even the real scholars, made students recite the textbook, verbatim. An eminent Yale historian's teaching, said one alumnus, "consisted simply in hearing the students repeat from memory the dates from Putz' *Ancient History*." He wondered how any part of the work of such a gifted man could be so "worthless."

This practice of rote recitation was gradually superseded—though it still survives surprisingly well in some academic quarters—by the introduction of the lecture. Young men who had studied in Germany risked their professional skins by importing this ultramodernism from overseas. In the early nineteenth century, a Dartmouth student wrote an enthusiastic letter home about a visit to Yale. He described a lecture on chemistry by the elder Benjamin Silliman, who presented a demonstration on combustion with the aid of a black servant acting as his laboratory assistant. But the lecture, too, is now widely denounced as an evil. It has been transcended by the seminar. Radicals like Henry Adams imported this vital teaching resource in the latter part of the last century. For his first seminar, Adams dared to ask the Harvard Librarian to set up a reserve shelf of books. Denied that absurdity, Adams asked the President to intervene.

Next, are our college and university studies becoming too impersonal and too detached from the life of our time? Deceived by optical illusion, many critics say yes. But what about the impersonality, detachment, and irrelevance of the nineteenth-century curriculum? It was focused on ancient Greece and Rome. As late as the 1870's, President McCosh of Princeton denounced modern history as "a let-off to easygoing students from the studies which require thought." The modern direction of the curriculum toward the recent past and increasingly toward the present, and its incipient major swing toward the future, gives it far more relevance and more comprehensiveness than it ever had.

The view of the erosion of our schools and colleges by permissiveness is still another fallacy caused by historical astigmatism. After writing *The Transformation of the School*, his brilliant study of educational progressivism from the 1870's to the

1940's, Professor Lawrence Cremin confessed that he had made one big mistake, visible in his title: there was no transformation. The progressive ideas, though much discussed, were not that much used. John Dewey, after suffering a half century of abuse for his radical views, asked, "Why doesn't somebody try them?"

Henry Seidel Canby, in his fine book *Alma Mater*, characterized our old campus experience as "strenuous idleness." Through brotherhood, service, and competition it was supposed to breed character. But requiring typically only an hour or so of study a day, against three or four today, it was rather easy on the head. Once last century the Williams College faculty decided to require a little more work. The students struck, even taking their protest to the New York papers. Our modern campus, permissive or not, appears to be breeding young people who want to study harder. A few years ago two undergraduate protests about work to reach the papers came from University of Wisconsin and Vanderbilt students asking for more.

During the late superheated criticism of our schools, the response of most secondary and elementary educators was to lie low. The many among them already trying or accomplishing important reforms expected rightly that they would be ignored in the storm; the diehards knew that they could ride it out. How can today's college and university educators prepare to weather *their* coming storm? Our faculty, though tireless critics of educators below them, may find it very difficult to endure searching criticism of themselves. There might be a sort of poetic justice in the spotlight's turning on them.

Their defensive tactics have been weak. Their usual recourse has been to use the red herring, that is, to distract attention from themselves by disparaging others—not only elementary and secondary school teachers but alumni, trustees, and—above all—administrators. Since the seventeenth century they have complained about the preparation of college candidates. "Where did anyone find these morons?" they grumble each fall. The Advanced Placement Program was instituted on the initiative of high schools whose graduates were finding their freshman year of college an anticlimax. The schools undertook with embarrassing success to offer some studies of college-fresh-

man level. In retaliation, instead of concentrating on improvement of their own freshman year and encouraging zealous
schoolteachers, many college and university faculty tried to
demonstrate that such threats to them from below did not
exist. As a clincher, they alleged that the schools were de-
teriorating.

Another means used by faculty to draw attention away from
their own shortcomings was the self-study. After World War
Two, foundations lavished money on college faculty so that
they might analyze their curriculum and teaching. The faculty
carried the analysis just far enough to make everyone feel conscientious and even a little adventurous, but not so far that
anyone thought he had to change anything. Few read the reports of self-studies. Their main effect was to reinforce the
*status quo.*

Lately, also, the faculty were trying to protect themselves
by extraenthusiastic participation in the wave of teach-ins.
Conniving at tragic and long-standing evils down the street
and at excruciating obsolescence on campus, they invited their
students to teach-ins over Vietnam. There they passionately
censured the government for its military sins, which are distant
and stark enough for easy simplification.

Will such distractions draw today's critics off the trail of the
professors? The hunt is up. Leaders of Middle America have
given the view halloo. State- and federal-education officialdom,
lately supporters of schoolteachers and principals, may not feel
so kindly toward the Olympian college professor. After running
with the hare, they may now switch and follow with the
hounds. Maybe businessmen, who stayed relatively quiet before, will join the field. Other groups, nursing pent-up aggres-
sion, may take it out in pursuit of such interesting quarry. Even
students may turn out and harass some of their more culpable
instructors.

The relevance and independence promised by some crusading faculty may appear to conservatives even more dangerous
than the intellectual buccaneering carried on in our most sophisticated high schools. Worse still for a nervous society,
many college faculty relish ambiguity and paradox and try to

stimulate students with heady draughts of irony. So if the better schoolteacher looked like a permissive Pied Piper, the better college teacher may look like another Socrates, luring young people away from honest work and trying "to make the worse appear the better reason." And if the intellectuals were outraged to find Life Adjustment being taught to underprivileged youngsters at Central High, how will they feel when they find Values taught to everybody at Parnassus U?

College faculty could safeguard themselves well by writing more good education history. Scholars have let this opportunity slip. Morison called the state of education history "a major scandal of American scholarship." He stumbled on it when undertaking a history of Harvard for her three-hundredth anniversary. He then qualified himself to criticize others by virtue of his own superb books about Harvard's three centuries. But little more education history of the best scholarly quality has been written, except by Rudolph, Cremin, Brubacher, Metzger, Hofstadter, and a few others. Very few.

A major effort by today's historians to reveal to the nation the tragicomedy of our educational past would improve today's image of our lower and higher schools together. Most of the serious faults of our education system are legacies from the past, not corruptions of the present. Our complaints should not be that schools and colleges have changed, but that they have not changed enough.

# 20 / Change

*After the Second World War, the Amherst College faculty*
*spent many months planning a new curriculum. In their book*
*about this project,* Education at Amherst, *they boasted that*
*virtually none of that time had been wasted in discussion of the*
*objectives of education.*

*"The real problem," they wrote, "is squeezing into the stu-*
*dent's working day all of the things we want him to do."*

"Drift, reluctant accommodation, and belated recognition
that while nobody was looking change has already taken place."
That's the description by Professor Frederick Rudolph, Williams College's historian of education, of how U.S. colleges
and universities have evolved. Except once. After the Civil
War, lasting, deep academic change did come at a pace that
was hardly brisk but perhaps resolute. Is that happening again?
By now, the conventionally educated person is coming to be
discredited by his ever more spectacular economic, social, and
political failures. Are we at one of those rare points when society demands something substantially new in education?

Scores of colleges, most of them small, independent, often
new, have tried bold academic reform during the last half

century. Their struggle was called the "progressive movement." Some of it caught on and spread widely; most of it petered out. But as a consequence of today's student revolt, the old progressive banner has been unfurled again, the big drum dusted off, the same crusade relaunched. This time will it succeed? Though professors lament how fragile, how precarious, higher education is, to me it seems as tough as the Pentagon. Its present bourgeois curriculum and pedagogy may survive for decades, as did the classical and Calvinist education of the old-time college. Students fought that for seventy-five years with a violence that ours have only recently begun to match. Will our system respond any sooner?

The first modern wave of reform began at Princeton before World War One. In the English manner, President Woodrow Wilson hired a staff of urbane young intellectuals as "preceptors." They supervised all the Tigers in some independent study. After the war, the movement spread far and wide, still mostly in imitation of Oxford and Cambridge. A traveler in Britain described those two universities at that time as "crawling" with American observers. They tried to transplant the genial scholarliness they'd seen—books, good talk, sherry, and cricket, all reinforcing each other.

Swarthmore imported the "honors" feature of the old British universities for an elite group of upperclassmen. Honors candidates took far fewer courses, and near graduation they were examined by faculty from other colleges. The Swarthmore faculty, spared the chore of testing and marking their students, could teach them with more freedom and warmth.

The cultivation of the gentleman-scholar went furthest at Harvard under an administrative genius, President Abbott Lawrence Lowell. He condemned both the sportsman and the bookworm as monsters. He aimed to foster a type of person as devoted to ideas as to fellowship. For this he established the House Plan. It was a powerful retaliation against our traditional narrowness. The Houses, each with its own dining room, library, tutors, squash courts, athletic teams, counselors, and engaging idiosyncrasies, were to bring students and faculty together in a style of intimate gentility. It was a diplomatic masterpiece, because Lowell got the many millions of dollars it cost from a Yale man.

By the 1930's, native reforms were gathering momentum, many inspired by the ideas of John Dewey. At Bennington College the choice of studies was left to each student, but she could expect generous support and criticism from her professors. One New Year's Eve a friend offered me a blind date. "She's a Bennington freshman." "She's a what?" She was dark, a little distant, attractive. "What goes on up there at—ah—Brattleboro?" "At Bennington!" "Ah, yes. Well, what are you studying up there?" "Proust." He'd just been rediscovered by the arbiters of literary fashion. "Great. What else?" "Nothing else." "What were you studying before that?" "Nothing." "You mean to say that for a semester of college you've just read Marcel Proust?" "That's right." The band struck up "Auld Lang Syne," and we kissed.

In his experimental college at the University of Wisconsin during the 1930's, Alexander Meiklejohn was trying to combine informality with structure. A student's first two years were spent living and working in a small student-faculty unit. As a freshman he studied the arts and sciences as they had emerged in Greek culture, and as a sophomore he studied them in American culture. One alumnus tells me he worked especially hard on a part in *Lysistrata* his freshman year and on a study of French colonization of the North Central states area his sophomore year. To enhance these experiences, he took seminars with several of Wisconsin's mighty scholars and swam on her varsity team. Another graduate recalled that Meiklejohn encouraged a teaching method that deserves wider trial: biology taught by a historian, history by a biologist; astronomy taught by an art historian, art history by an astronomer. The specialist takes part in the discussion only as a consultant.

But the regulars on the Wisconsin faculty let the experimental college die when the university's powerful progressive president, Glenn Frank, was killed in an automobile accident. They have sabotaged experiments at improving higher education at other large universities. Some, like Chicago's Shimer or Columbia's Bard, have survived by splintering off and moving to the center. To the center also have moved most of the small independent ones.

Goddard is one of the exceptions. Located on a hillside in northern Vermont, this small, spirited college has been consistently trying to apply the principles of John Dewey since its progressive program was introduced in the 1930's. One of the buildings is named Dewey Hall. Goddard today appears to be as progressive as ever.

There a student may shape his own curriculum, but in frequent consultation with his professors he must penetrate deeply the field he chooses and relate it broadly to other fields. He carries out a yearly project off campus developed as much as possible from on-campus studies. At one time, as academic work, the English students produced a newspaper for the local townspeople. This project was a course, listed in the catalogue. For another course, the drama students took an Elizabethan play on an extensive tour of high schools throughout the state. Today all are encouraged to spend one of their college years studying in India or in another such drastically different society. One reason why Goddard could keep going in this unconventional way has been thirty years of powerful direction by President Royce Pitkin. A Vermont sage, he resembles Will Rogers in face and style. The students addressed him as "Tim."

While Goddard moved forward, St. John's College of Annapolis moved backward to what its leaders proudly called "medieval education." The objective: such a balanced, integrated, cosmopolitan, common intellectual experience as bred Dante and Saint Thomas Aquinas. All students take the same program all four years, with no electives and no major. They read and discuss in seminars the 100 or so books that have most deeply influenced the culture of man. As at Wisconsin, the faculty trade around the teaching of their specialties, if they have one. St. John's was founded in the eighteenth century. Appropriately, everybody studies Greek among the neoclassical buildings, and in conversation some students sound a little like participants in a dialogue of Plato. The strength of this experimental program, introduced like Goddard's in the 1930's, was dramatically proven in 1964 when the college reproduced itself. Another St. John's now offers the same education in Santa Fe, New Mexico. It has recently been the recipient of a sizable grant from the Ford Foundation for more adventuring in neomedieval education.

Black Mountain College in North Carolina set the highwater mark of experiment. The site chosen for it was a far-off spot in the Blue Ridge, "the oldest mountains on earth," the catalogue boasted in graceful irony. There, in the 1930's the banner of academic revolution was planted. The college's offerings, principles, and style ranged over the entire spectrum of progressive education. When students and faculty joined together to construct some of the college buildings, they reached a prime goal of progressivism—the head and the hand serving each other. *Life* magazine gave Black Mountain a big, exciting spread, and intellectuals chattered about it over Martinis. The catalogue was the only one in thousands worth reading, and the forerunners of today's campus radicals applied, went, and often stayed on. For a bachelor's degree? Phooey! None was offered. You stayed until you'd learned something. Some splendid education took place, some not so splendid. By the 1950's, isolation, eccentricity, and lack of cash were demoralizing all hands. As word spread of drastic crises with walkouts of large parties of faculty and students, the institution appeared to be fibrillating, as the doctors say. In the late 1950's I met a college candidate from New York who had asked around the city about Black Mountain. Nobody knew much. He wrote for a catalogue and application. No answer. When he went down by bus to the nearby North Carolina town and inquired, the local loafers reckoned maybe there was a college up yonder. He climbed a hill and found some attractive buildings, but no sign of life except smoke coming out of the chimney of one house. It was a caretaker's. The crisis had passed, and Black Mountain was dead. It had played the finest scene in an early act of the continuing tragicomedy of progressive education.

Such experimentation in the 1930's might have vitalized U.S. higher education if World War Two and then our post-Sputnik conniptions had not provoked a reactionary academic spasm. Discipline the intellect! Train the specialist! Also, other educators were put off by "progressive Bohemianism," as it was then called. They were more shocked by the bare feet of a student entering the library than awed by the wheelbarrowful of books he was returning. Furthermore, most of the country's educators could go on with their routine with a better conscience, because a few were practicing heroic innovations, just as an indifferent Christian may feel easier knowing that while he sins a monk is praying.

Seminal ideas can surface dramatically from unexpected sources. By the mid-1950's, the influence of the postwar hyper-scholastics was reaching its climax; traditionalism appeared to be triumphing; reactionaries were promoting foreign languages and mathematics for their disciplinary effect—the crime that crippled Latin and Greek; in some school systems McGuffey's readers were being purchased again. During this conservative panic, a powerful declaration of the most basic progressivism was heard from a nonconformist industrial leader, Edwin Land, founder and president of the Polaroid Corporation. As a trustee of the Massachusetts Institute of Technology, Dr. Land was focusing his unorthodox imagination upon higher education. He reminded educators that problems teach better than solutions. He proposed a basic change, in a paper for the academic community entitled "A Time for Greatness." To stimulate fulfillment in young people, Land made this proposal: let students work not on the known, as they usually do now, but on the unknown; let them help the faculty wrestle with issues in the excitement of exploration on the frontier of scholarship; and let them work close to their professors, not in the classroom or in conventional laboratory periods, but on the faculty's own projects.

I'm told Dr. Land became an academic radical when he found he could not help his daughter with her junior-high-school algebra until he threw away her textbook. And I hear his radical emotions flared higher still when the idea for instantly developing color photography, another Polaroid breakthrough, came to a born inventor Land had hired after he met the man pumping gas in a service station.

A few years ago I asked an administrator at MIT how much of Dr. Land's dream had come true there. He smiled wryly. "You know how universities *love* to change." I also know how the world would love to cope with cohorts of young people prepared for greatness.

Land's dream does appear to have come true at one spot in the interface between the university and the universe: the Wright Institute, located in Berkeley, California. Jerry, a senior, came in last spring for information about something new and better. He wanted advanced study in sociology, but he did not want to be locked into the behavioral-science establishment. What's wrong with the establishmentarians? He says he's suffered too much already under their hodgepodge of technique and theory: the influence of ideology on sampling error, or the development of functionalism since William Graham Sumner. These are interesting and important topics but cloying to him as a steady diet. He wants to be closer to the population and their human feelings. Jerry's blue eyes flashed rather formidably over his red beard as he looked at me for information. How about applying to the Wright Institute? What's that? It's a place for the study of problems. It's the behavioral-science underground come out from under. It was founded in the early 1960's by Dr. Nevitt Sanford after he spent several years in intensive study of college students, faculty, and curriculum. He put some proposals for drastic reform in a book, *Where Colleges Fail* (1967). He argues that higher education will improve only when we add to our training of the intellect a far better education of the personality.

Dr. Sanford is a very handsome man. He speaks with a slightly Southern accent. Like Secretary Hickel, he has a large family who share their ideas with him, often enough anyway. His interest in the reform of higher education was aroused in the late 1940's when faculty in California were singled out for a loyalty oath. This has since been declared unconstitutional. But Sanford was struck at the time by the poor morale this event revealed in professors. Though vehemently opposed to the act, they soon surrendered to it almost totally. Why? Sanford began to suspect this was a symptom of something radically wrong with our colleges and universities. They are too disjointed, too remote. In a word, too impersonal.

How can the qualities of humanity be brought out in faculty and students? Dr. Sanford thinks Freud's ideas can still serve. Over his breakfast coffee at an educational conference, he mused about Freud. He's either slavishly followed or impatiently rejected. Too bad. He's the strongest voice yet calling people to respect their sound impulses, sharpen their sense of self, toughen their conscience. "Those three things our academic system actually discourages."

Nevitt Sanford acts as well as he talks and writes. He gathered scholars and students at his Institute to attack the three most dangerous causes of academic inhumanity: futility, compartmentalization, and skimpy teaching. The attack has three prongs: one, a search for direct, practical solutions to urgent, baffling problems; two, a drawing together of workers in a wide variety of disciplines; three, constant, generous teaching of the younger members by the older.

So Jerry pictured himself in the Institute, first, as a graduate sociology student working in an investigation, say, of unemployment. His findings would be used directly by legislators, governors, mayors, counselors, clergy, businessmen. Second, in the Peaceable Kingdom of the Institute he sees how the psychology lion must lie down with him, the sociology lamb, or even with fellow beasts from economics, anthropology, law, business administration, or maybe even a creature from that professional field that all good behavioral scientists despise— social work. Third, he dreams of himself laboring away at the elbow of master scholars.

Jerry wrote off at once to the Institute. He brought back good news, too. It must be in fine shape: for entrance in the fall of 1970, fifteen applicants were competing for every opening.

Can our vast system grow and thus avoid a long period of torpor punctuated with protest, more or less violent? If so, will such growth be enhanced through following successful independent experiments, like Goddard and St. John's, and through stepping up new versions of them, such as New College, Old Westbury, Potomac, Sangamon, Santa Cruz, Hampshire? In the mid-1960's, I visited the "Free University" on Fourteenth Street in New York City. It offered a heavily Marxist curriculum. It was held together by a shoestring. Is it still open? This second generation of pioneers is going over old ground and refighting earlier battles, but maybe now it can win them. Does it stand a better chance of winning them in the 1970's?

Or will the system grow through novel units set within existing universities, like the one begun at Columbia in the fall of 1970? A few dozen men and women undergraduates lived and studied in quarters in a hotel fifteen blocks down Broadway from the university. On the principle that they will learn better if their classes are not separate from their social life, they study, discuss, fraternize, eat, and sleep in a sort of academic commune headed last year by Kate Millett. A similar community, Bensalem College, is attached to Fordham University and set up in an apartment house across the street from the Rose Hill campus. With extraordinary responsibility for deciding on what, when, how, and even where they study, Bensalem students are promised a Fordham B.A. degree in three years. When I visited last year, a half dozen of them, with one instructor, had just moved out and settled on City Island to initiate a project about which the rest could not yet tell me much. A project of some others, who stayed put, was the planning, organizing, and teaching of an elementary school. By himself, one young man was taking all the courses in ontology offered by the regular Fordham faculty of philosophy.

The state universities of Vermont and Connecticut in the 1970–1971 academic year sprouted official experimental colleges, too. I've known of Connecticut's only through an article on the food page of the New York *Times*. A member of the faculty was shown teaching students how to prepare rock Cornish hen by a French recipe. But the most telling sign of general academic obsolescence is the hatching of unofficial experimental "free colleges" from smaller institutions, such as Reed College, which were supposed to be experimental anyway.

Or will the breakthrough come in a major change within the regular college program of an old university like Brown, in Rhode Island? During the fall of 1969, word came down from Providence that this distinguished Ivy League institution was committed to an all-college reform. Marks and required courses had been abandoned, students were allowed to design majors unrecognizable to traditionalists, and a sort of course new at Brown was invented: Modes of Thought. One such course in science, A Study of Optimization, was devoted to the design of a yacht. No technical prerequisites; enrollment limited to good sailors.

Who knows? The independent experiments could fail to weather the Recession and its consequences. Budget deficits, drugs, and outside hostility are threatening our stronger colleges; they might snuff out these precarious ventures. They may also fly apart from the centrifugal force they generate.

The affiliated experimental colleges could fail for the same reasons. Columbia's commune has moved from the hotel to a mansion by the Hudson, with a gorgeous view of the George Washington Bridge. But some participants fear they haven't "gotten it together" well enough. Bensalem could follow. Only a couple of years ago Fordham abandoned another experimental program at its Lincoln Center campus in Manhattan, over the protests of outraged students, who held a sit-in, and some faculty, who charged a betrayal by reactionary colleagues.

The new Brown program, developed under the leadership of students, also looks precarious. This was a fine example of student power, peacefully applied to that sensitive area as yet unprobed by the main thrust of white campus revolution—academic exploitation in the classroom. But though the chief Brown reformer, Ira Magaziner, of New York City, is a brilliant young evangelist, still he was not only just a student, he was about to graduate. In fact, he did graduate the spring before his plan was to be implemented. Will this unprofessional and casually led reform be allowed to stand and grow?

I believe even the collegiate experiments that die out leave seeds that lie buried in the soul of education, like acorns in the soil. Wisconsin's new Liberal Integrated College reads in the catalogue as though it had sprung from Meiklejohn's experimental college. Columbia alone in the Ivy League is trying a splinter college, perhaps because some dim memory of its affiliation with Bard College has survived in the psyche of the Columbia Community. And Brown's effort at massive change could be traced to a recessive institutional gene buried since early last century. Then, Brown's president, Francis Wayland, led the progressives of that day against an army of hostile puritan educators. All the themes of the current revolution of campus youth spring from the long tradition of the progressive movement in education.

If academia cannot respond, our present colleges and universities may have to be abandoned and left as picturesque relics of once great institutions, like the English monasteries disestablished by King Henry VIII. Television could take their pedagogical place as Sesame Street is supposed to take the place of our elementary-reading teachers for vast numbers of black children. New private commercial corporations could take the place of our higher academic institutions, as they have already done, for teaching certain elementary skills, in several public-school systems. Certainly the research function now carried on widely in the academic world could be taken over by nonacademic institutions, as it was in seventeenth-century Europe when the universities had become too rigid and inane for distinguished scholarship. During the colonial period, the small number of active scholars on our faculties had to establish themselves by correspondence with the Royal Society in London. Even in the 1930's, Dr. Abraham Flexner founded the Institute for Advanced Studies in Princeton—not as part of the university—because he had despaired of our universities as centers for dynamic culture. Indeed, I know an unusually productive young scholar, very successful in his acquiring of grants and other backing for his own work, who nevertheless may leave his university and take part in the founding of an institute of the seventeenth-century sort. It might be an American branch representing a European institute he has already joined.

But the incendiary campus rebels, though vicious in means, give the clearest testimony to the obsolescence of higher education. After a predawn explosion ripped the Army Mathematics Research Center at the University of Wisconsin and professors and students were sifting through the ruins of their laboratories, one of them wondered "whether universities are still a place for serious research."

Education history teaches that such catastrophes are a sign of the folly not so much of activist young people as of their lazy elders. But maybe the slow way is not only the way we do it but the best way. After finishing his ten-volume *Story of Civilization*, Will Durant mused thus, in a magazine article, about the pace of change:

It is good that new ideas should be heard, for the sake of the few that can be used; but it is also good that new ideas should be compelled to go through the mill of objection, opposition, and contumely; this is the trial heat which innovations must survive before being allowed to enter the human race. The trial heat may also familiarize society with the innovations so they can be taken up, when their time comes, without traumatic shock.

# 21 / U.S.A.

*Could the state of U.S. education be like the state of a nu-
clear process just before the energy is released? The point of
"critical mass" has almost been reached. The materials still sit
inert. Then one more small item is added. . . .*

George Washington rode horseback with his stepson, Jackie
Custis, and a servant all the way from Virginia to New York
to enroll Custis at Columbia. Like many successful men without formal education, Washington craved it for his children.
Although Jackie's interests at the time were horses and girls,
a famous schoolmaster in Alexandria had prodded him through
some of Cicero's orations and a few Greek verbs and kept him
out of the local taverns. Washington didn't think much of the
country's colleges. But he had been assured that Columbia
was the best. President Myles Cooper promised to keep a special watch on the young man, and the servant was instructed
to do what he could. Unfortunately, the project failed. Custis
dropped out, and his stepfather's reservations about our higher
education remained.

Maybe Jackie would have taken to the study of agriculture. Washington was fascinated by that science. He came to agree with Dr. Benjamin Rush, of Philadelphia, whose article in *The American Museum*, in 1787, urged a national university that would raise teaching quality and introduce practical subjects such as agriculture. At the Constitutional Convention, Washington joined with those who wanted a provision for a federally financed and directed university; in his Farewell Address he made an appeal for one; and in his will he left a bequest to help support it.

The next five U.S. Presidents were also for a national university, and three formally proposed it to the Congress. Presidents Grant and Hayes tried again. These men were disappointed by the mediocrity of our colleges, most of which resembled modern boarding schools going through a period of low morale. At the same time, they were impressed by the distinguished national universities in Paris and Berlin. But too many Americans considered federal intervention in education worse than mediocrity. They also feared the European intellectuals who would have to be imported as faculty. In 1814, President Timothy Dwight of Yale warned that "they would not be Christians but Edinburgh Reviewers—men who would throw religion out of the world with one stroke." Worst of all, too many feared Washington as a location for a university —a place, as Billy Graham calls it today, too sinful and irreligious for young people.

As a consequence of these fears, we have no national university. And yet federal money has been spent generously for our higher education. And 100 years ago, when the academic system was in deep trouble, the Congress gave it not only massive financial support but leadership as well.

By the middle of the last century, our colleges had become too stagnant to survive. Their studies were a worn-out ritual dominated by the classics, and their pedagogy was based on daily recitation of memorized material. "We were expected to wade through Homer as though the *Iliad* were a bog." Such bored students were protesting with riot and arson, enrollments stood still against a rising population, and faculty and alumni fought off reform. Only a powerful outside force could save the system.

At about the same time, Oxford and Cambridge had become stagnant, too—their curriculum, teaching methods, and admissions arrangements having changed very little since the mid-Renaissance. Dogged faculty backed up by sentimental alumni warded off attempts at reform until the British Parliament through legislation finally forced them to modernize.

Encouraged by the British example, the Congress struck, too. In 1862, it passed the Morrill Act. This act had been promoted for several years with granite firmness by Vermont's Congressman Justin Morrill. After a Buchanan veto, it was finally enacted and signed by Abraham Lincoln. The Morrill Act, through gifts to the states of national lands for the founding of land-grant colleges, financed free higher education in "agriculture and the mechanical arts," along with the liberal arts. This breakthrough triggered both an enrollment explosion and the only major curriculum reform in U.S. educational history.

A Yale student of the Class of 1863 looked into a chemistry laboratory and saw another student examining a colored liquid in a glass tube. A feeling of wonder came over him, he said, and then of disgust "that any human being should give his time to pursuits so futile." But by the 1880's, experimental science was so firmly established in the curriculum that humanities faculty thought their studies were being overwhelmed by it. A Columbia professor of classics used this metaphor: "The perfume of the Attic violet is being stifled by the stench of the chemist's crucible."

The Morrill Act appears the most important single force in the opening up of the curriculum. For when mining, architecture, and home economics had broken the academic monopoly of the classics, dozens of other new studies could at last find a place in the curriculum. So when Tom, Dick, and Harry came to college, they could be offered not only technical and professional courses but modern languages, literature, social studies, and laboratory science. The land-grant colleges were the educational expression of Henry Clay's idea, "the American system," a grand campaign of expansion and diversification of our transportation, industry, and invention.

Like Clay, Morrill had had only elementary schooling. By the age of forty-five, he had succeeded in business and farming well enough to devote himself to politics. He then served as a Congressman and Senator for forty-three years with such distinction that he was called "the American Gladstone." Besides the Land-Grant Acts he was chiefly responsible for legislation promoting the Library of Congress. One of the colleges of Michigan State University has recently been named for him.

The colleges set up by the Morrill Act were given a free hand in designing their academic programs. Besides adding practical studies to the classical and other liberal arts studies, their only other requirement was to offer military training. According to the President of Cornell in the 1870's, this was not for defense against foreign enemies but against domestic "Communists and demagogues." Still, it was not required of students. So without bothersome federal control—the old American nightmare—Washington had helped resuscitate academia.

Today academia is suffering a paralysis. Washington seems concerned. In the late 1960's, a chorus of criticism kept coming from President Johnson's highest education officers. John Gardner, the Secretary of Health, Education, and Welfare, described our colleges and universities as "floundering." He condemned the narrow focus and triviality of what too many scholars study and teach. He also complained that they inoculate their students with an "anti-leadership vaccine." That is, college faculties are subtly dissuading students from acquiring skill or interest in the new kind of leadership required to humanize our bureaucracy, and they even subvert belief in the need for any sort of leadership. Johnson's Commissioner of Education, Harold Howe, warned the assembled American Association of University Professors that the country can no longer tolerate the widening gap between their brilliant achievements in specialized research and their failure as educators. Then in 1968 the President's National Security Council knocked graduate students out of their special draft deferment and into the top of the order of induction. This was a warning: the government has no reverence for today's academic system and doesn't mind using shock treatment for educators.

After hearing the disparagement from Lyndon Johnson's staff, one could even read into the order canceling graduate-student deferment a warning to colleges and universities: prepare not more scholars but better educators.

How concerned is the Nixon Administration? At first, the President dwelt on discipline, telling the U.S. Chamber of Commerce that college educators should control their students "with more backbone." At the same time, his Justice Department leaders were calling some campus rebels "ideological criminals." But then the Administration began to pick out other targets. Secretary Finch, then of HEW, dubbed the tenured faculty "one of the most privileged classes on earth," from whose exploitation students should have better protection. Finally, in May, 1969, the President was shown a speech about the general failure of our higher learning, delivered by University of Michigan Professor Stephen J. Tonsor to the National Association of Manufacturers. This historian described both faculty and staff of our colleges and universities as opportunist and even subtly anti-intellectual. He branded Alma Mater a poorly paid prostitute who rejects her own students in their academic need and offers herself to government and industry for technical services she should not be performing anyway.

Tonsor offered a striking proposal: let the federal government give much less money to universities and their faculties and give much more directly to students. The President may have encountered this proposal in 1969 in two places: one was a solemn report by a Carnegie commission appointed to examine the financing of higher education; the other a cavalier article by Irving Kristol in *The New York Times Magazine*. Both argued that students can best exert pressure for academic reform if given greater financial power; a college will offer new academic goods only in a buyer's market where a student with tuition money may choose his college more warily.

But this idea apparently did not win over the President until he encountered it in Professor Tonsor's speech. He commended

the proposal and Tonsor's whole point of view as very close
to his own, sent a copy to all his Administration leaders, and
directed them to follow it in any public comments in higher
education. They should ignore, as Mr. Nixon put it, "the tut-
tut they would surely hear from the establishment"—a faction
from which some college students may be relieved to learn
the President of the United States dissociates himself.

But money alone can't cause fundamental change. Educational leadership is also needed. A catalyst must be added. In
Justin Morrill's project, it was new academic subject matter.
Most post-World War Two and post-Sputnik Congressional
financial support has succeeded in promoting only more of the
same tired nineteenth-century education. In the late 1940's and
early 1950's, the government did give more than 3 million
veterans many billions of dollars to help them attend their
chosen colleges. But no proposal for educational reform was
attached to the financial support. So no academic improvement
other than a rise in general standards came from its impact.
Professor Ernest Earnest described that rise in *Academic Procession,* his history of American colleges and universities. He
and his colleagues at first condescended to the World War
Two veteran for his opportunism, then felt a threat in his
aggressiveness, and finally—seeing a challenge in his seriousness
—took more pains with teaching and course content. One
Columbia professor says he is still kept on his toes by the
memory of an impatient veteran who threatened to beat him
up. But the faculty have managed to hold their academic system of curriculum and teaching otherwise intact, warding off
threats of reform.

Wanted: a Justin Morrill with a catalytic academic idea. He
will be a Senator or Congressman of political genius and deep
concern for the reform of higher education. He will perceive,
again, some critically important fields of study now outlawed
from the college curriculum. He will count the multitudes of
young people who need them. He will lead the Congress to a
radical piece of legislation that will enable those young people
to undertake those studies.

I expect that his new academic program will advance two

new fields, among others: first, it will advance creative art; second, it will advance the study of the future.

The government has lent generous support to the arts before. Only a generation ago, a New Deal Congress invested huge sums of money and enlisted much imaginative leadership for projects for unemployed actors, painters, sculptors, musicians, and writers. Bold experiment took place, as in Hallie Flanagan's productions for the Federal Theatre Project, which opened the way to a revolution on the American stage. In the economic depression of the 1930's, thousands of artists had to be rescued from physical starvation. In the educational bankruptcy of the 1970's, millions of college students will need to be rescued from spiritual starvation.

In 1970, President Nixon asked the Congress to quadruple the appropriation for the National Foundation on the Arts and the Humanities. His chief reason: in a time of heightened friction among people at home and abroad our greatest need is better communication. The arts can train us in that more effectively than any other means. The President may have noted George Bernard Shaw's remark about the power of art. It was quoted by a dancer who testified at one of the appropriation bill's hearings: "Art persuades faster than anything except torture."

Higher education has been steadily shifting toward the study of the future of our society in this world. A medieval student argued over whether faith or reason was the better way to the next one. A Renaissance student read Plutarch's *Lives of the Noble Greeks and Romans*. A modern student learns about the ideas of Keynes, Einstein, or Freud concerning men and things here and now. Progressive educators suggest that he examine them himself.

The next logical step is to move on up into the future. Just the sort of academic innovation for another Morrill Act! It should seem no more drastic than the change from Latin and Greek to Bunsen burners and business cycles. Like the technical education introduced by Morrill, "future" education equips young people to do something. Scholarship in this field now tends to develop alternate futures from which students may choose one and work to bring it into being. The field includes much research into values. The majority of futurists are said to be optimists.

Furthermore, faculty prepared to teach the future are probably somewhat more numerous now than faculty prepared to teach technology were in Morrill's day. In the 1970's, a college president can draw on a larger pool of teachers who know trend extrapolation, cross-impact analysis, and objective trees than the pool of teachers his predecessor in the 1870's could draw on who knew soil sampling, spectrum analysis, and the uses of the power lathe. Dr. John McHale, a sociologist and designer, surveyed the field of futures research for the government. He estimates 600 full-time and 500 part-time workers in it. Professor H. Wentworth Eldredge, who teaches courses in the future at Dartmouth College, estimates that about seventy-five such courses are now offered in North America. About 100 faculty are involved. He sees two general types among them, both valuable: younger, student-oriented professors in the social sciences and humanities, using a wide variety of research and teaching techniques, who are out to "bust" the *status quo;* older professors in the natural sciences, business, and engineering, pedagogically conservative, inclined toward quantitative methods, some of them consultants for industry and government.

Among the younger futurists and their students research has been concentrated, I gather, on such areas as the future of the city, the family, privacy, peace, sex, life styles, aging, the mind, the universe; among the older, on forecasting in such areas as politics, business, economic resources, man power, pollution, and problem solving.

But all need rich creativity. Futurism and art meet in pursuit of that. They meet obviously in such methods of the futurists as scenario building, simulation gaming, dynamic modeling, interviewing, values analysis, role playing, and disciplined speculation. More important, they meet in the service they must both perform: helping us to learn how better to build, change, and renew.

Here are three projects, each for a term's work in a futurist curriculum, each for a team of students and faculty:

1. Plan the movement of all manufacturing to the moon. Include persons especially interested in machinery working under less gravity, in disposal of pollutants, in joint financing by all nations, in popular promotion of the idea, in its presentation to legislators, in its effects on our lives.

2. Explore the merits of specializing cities more thoroughly and better: New York for communication, Chicago for commerce, Detroit for transportation, Boston for research, Las Vegas for fun, Washington for ceremony. Suggest other cities for specialization.

3. Examine and evaluate several past utopias, and relate them to the whole culture of their time. Then project a new one from emerging realities today.

The federal government has always invested its dollars in higher education for a specific purpose of importance to the nation as a whole—such as for improved farming, defense, school guidance—or for the benefit of some group in the nation needing special help—such as veterans or blacks. The second great academically seminal act of the Congress could well be the founding of colleges for the study of art and the future. These would benefit the nation, as did the land-grant colleges, by challenging and jostling our present academic system into new growth. They would enormously benefit those various groups who cannot adapt to our present middle-class, masculine, oververbal, inflexible curriculum. And they would lead the rest of higher education into the direct preparation of young people to help "forge . . . the uncreated conscience of our race."

# 22 / Art

*"Just look," the instructor commanded me, waving his arm around the studio in a wide sweep. "Look at them, will you. Every single one of those pictures is as unique as the student who painted it. Look at that one. And that one. And that one." He strode over and picked one up and held it out as though I might see it better.*

"I'm taking a course in sculpture," Bill volunteers when we meet on College Walk. By the end of sophomore year, he's become an adept student and a varsity-football wheel horse. You'd think he'd consolidate those gains for a while. But now he has a new look—a bit insurgent, if not subversive. On his head he sports a tam-o'-shanter, at his throat a loud silk scarf.

Why sculpture? "Because it helps me cope. It gets me away from all those abstractions." Bill gestures impatiently toward a classroom building. In an academic climate polluted with too many words, he now works with things; from lecture halls quarantined against deep feeling he escapes into a studio pervaded with it. Whereas another student pores over books to prepare for the future, Bill sculpts for present satisfaction. Whereas others learn for their own benefit, he learns in order to share his insights, perhaps even with a crowded gallery.

The number of such revolutionaries is growing, and they are a greater threat to the academic establishment than are those who seize buildings and rough up administrators. Quietly turning from the traditional subjects to take courses in sculpture, painting, dance, film, drama, music, and writing, they are changing our colleges and universities at their core—the curriculum.

"Man must learn to live aesthetically or cease to be man—cease to be, that is, an animal who responds meaningfully to challenge. Everyone must some day become an artist—or a saint." This pronouncement came last year from Eric Larrabee, Provost of the State University of New York at Buffalo. Art, he predicted, will soon replace science at the center of higher education. Past experience supports him: grand academic reforms occur after crises like today's, when events are heady, students wrought up, and faculty extramonkish.

The curriculum has undergone three revolutions since the universities were created 1,000 years ago. The first was from the simple grammatical studies of the Dark Ages to the theology and argument of medieval Scholasticism ("Can angels converse with men?"); the second, in the Renaissance, to that revival of ancient authors and worship of words called "classicism" ("How did Cicero say it?"); and the third, to late nineteenth-century scientism and the reign of analysis ("Do the data fit the hypothesis?").

At each overthrow, a radical new academic subject transformed the others. In the Middle Ages, it was logic; in the Renaissance, ancient literature; in the nineteenth century, science. By now not only has that latest intruder overrun the colleges, but the social studies and humanities have even copied it. Their scholars try to be objective and cool; they try to explain things by counting them, if possible, or at least by analyzing them. But too much emphasis on counting and analysis kills. Already it has paralyzed the system of higher education. To revive it, another revolution is now brewing. Faculty and students will turn from the analysis of culture to the making of it. Scientism will give way to creativity. The new radicalizing subject will be art.

In America how is academic revolution accomplished? We have had only one example—the replacement, a century ago, of the classics by the sciences. A few progressive faculty started it. Next, many students joined in. Finally, half a dozen college presidents took command.

In the Renaissance, men like Petrarch had shown that the ancient pagan authors could help rejuvenate a tired Europe, but the first American educators imported the classical studies not so much for the wit of Horace, the romance of Virgil, the passion of Sophocles as for the tough discipline of learning Latin and Greek. A few educators, like Ezra Stiles, President of Yale in the late eighteenth century, triggered the scientific reaction against this misdirected classicism. Though a conservative theologian, Stiles was a progressive scientist who did original work in astronomy and meteorology. He even instructed his young men about electricity, using a spark generated in a contraption sent him by Benjamin Franklin.

Then students stepped up the revolt, often violently. For some reason, the Princetonians were the most violent. During the first half of the nineteenth century, they several times occupied Nassau Hall, barricading the building and defending it against all comers, including the town constables, with a missile arsenal of Latin dictionaries and chamber pots. Once, the students paraded in front of Nassau armed with dirks and firearms.

But the academic revolution was at its most formidable in the students' own scientific and literary societies. On many campuses, the young men were as creative as they were violent. A visitor to Haverford College during the 1860's might expect an invitation to an evening session of the Loganian Society by members sporting elegant club badges. He would hear the chairman ask the committees on botany, mineralogy, zoology, and entomology for their monthly reports on field work and experiments. That night, an enthusiastic Loganian might ring the college bell at 4 A.M. to rouse all Haverfordians to watch a meteor shower the astronomy committee was mapping.

Most faculty fearfully guarded the curriculum against such impiety. Nature should be approached to glorify God's handiwork, not to discover upsetting new facts. In the 1870's, an Amherst biologist could still be banned by his colleagues from further science teaching because for several weeks he kept his students eagerly dissecting the clam. As today, a few creative presidents were needed, strong enough to be champions of drastic change. The Harvard trustees found one first in a thirty-five-year-old chemistry professor, Charles W. Eliot, who was a match for any faculty Goliath. Several other major universities were soon headed by irresistible progressives. By the end of the century, laboratory science was being taught in all but the most pious colleges.

Under the influence of science, the entire curriculum has been broken up into narrow specialties. Though young people are eager to learn how to relate the liberal arts to one another, faculties today offer knowledge in chunks—philosophy, anthropology, astronomy, economics. They require students to take each chunk in almost complete isolation from any other chunk. A young man told me of a dream in which he lay on an operating table, where his professors, the better to teach him their subjects, were carving him into sections.

Furthermore, science has reached into all other fields and tempted scholars to overindulge in analysis. For example, during the last two or three decades, English faculties have lionized Henry James. The complicated life and work of this fastidious expatriate can be elegantly analyzed: On how many levels do James's symbols operate? Does psychology or melodrama predominate in his novels? Was his rejection of his country really a rejection of his father? Can the stylistic complexity of his later work be attributed to his dictating it? By such unromantic inquiry humanists would emulate chemists.

Also, the objectivity of the scientist has been all too contagious. When imitated by scholars in other fields, it degenerates into timidity. Society asks heroic questions: Why do blacks riot? Why does money inflate? Why has alcoholism spread? Academic scholars are expected to suggest answers, but they can't because too much of what they know is, as David Riesman says, "on a plateau of low-level abstraction, neither concrete enough for reality-testing nor conceptual and detached enough for philosophical reorientation."

Finally, pseudo science has aggravated the old American academic vice of continually testing and marking students. It destroys their zest. "Why withdraw from English 3306?" I asked another student. "I see Shaw's plays on the reading list," he replied, "and I want to enjoy them." "But why withdraw?" "Oh, come on," he reproached me, "with midterms, finals, and a term paper? And a mark?" Like him, too many students turn off. They will turn on again when another subject liberates higher education. The only one now ready to do so is art.

Art has been on the campuses for a long time. Students performed music in colonial days, as when President Witherspoon brought his bride back to Princeton and an instrumental ensemble serenaded the pair from the belfry of Nassau Hall. For a few decades before the Civil War, college histories record a growth of student art, probably influenced by John Ruskin and the Pre-Raphaelites. According to historian Frederick Rudolph, students in the 1850's founded, organized, and financed the museum that still flourishes at Williams College. In addition to providing a collection of masters, they displayed their own work, including the design of a gymnasium for the college.

At length, the arts were allowed into the curriculum—reluctantly. In 1874, the Harvard catalogue announced two new courses for undergraduates: one a studio course in drawing and painting, the other art history "as related to literature." The studio did not flourish. Until today, at Harvard and elsewhere, candidates for the liberal arts bachelor's degree have been allowed only a few credits for studio work. If they want more, they are urged, often condescendingly, to enroll in a professional art school.

But art history has prospered. It is bookish; it can be analyzed and talked about by scholars. Students can be set to reading and writing about it. It has been made into a specialty, and few artists teach it. One sculptor who does said to me of his art-history colleagues, "They hate art." They admit it to their departmental curriculum only if it is emasculated. A liberal arts student can study, even major in, musicology or dra-

matic literature, but he can get little or no academic credit
for taking music or drama. He can, indeed, use the new art
facilities, containing studios, practice rooms, and theaters, if
he attends Marietta, Harvard, St. Lawrence, Birmingham-
Southern, and hundreds of other colleges. He can even study
under real artists. But he soon perceives that the general faculty, as well as the art historians, musicologists, and professors
of dramatic literature, jim-crow these intruders and refuse to
recognize as academically meaningful the creative work they
direct. I once heard an eminent musicologist snort with contempt over the growing enrollment of string players at his
university's conservatory.

This pride will have its fall as more students, their eyes
opened by the campus revolution to the artificiality of traditional studies, rediscover creative art. Some already see it not
as an academic option but as a revolutionary act. After Columbia's first "bust," a student changed his program from doctoral work in history to master's work in painting. "I began to
resent all those learned, witty men condescending to me." At
the same time, an undergraduate majoring in political science re-
scheduled his senior year to include all the work he could get
credit for in sculpture. He chose to study welding, a technique
that has become very popular among college art students.
One of his pieces was displayed in a show sponsored by the
School of the Arts. It is a crucifixion—its material, automobile
springs.

When denied art as academic work, students get it on their
own. They found societies, not only to show but to make films.
At some large universities they present three or four dozen
plays each year. They publish scores of magazines of poetry
and fiction. College newspapers run series by student photographers who try to catch the moods of people and the grace of
things around college. Seniors replace the Edwardian material
of the usual yearbook with Aquarian art and writing.

Even campus confrontation can be theater, if not dance.
A crowd of protesters in their buckskin jackets, obsolete military uniforms, beads, headbands, striped bell bottoms, battered
top hats, and boots does look like the cast of an opera. One

journalist called such demonstrations "the choreography of confrontation." Campus protest is a challenge to our society to improve. It is a demand by young people for power. Even more, it is an expression of their need for new roles, new forms, new styles.

On or off campus, this generation is resourceful in finding outlets for protest against the corruption they think they see in American culture. They transcend it: into drugs or Canada; into science-fiction and fantasy literature; or onto a motorcycle —today's counterpart for Pegasus. They retaliate: with the romance of rock music; with expert draft counseling; or with the ritualistic sacking of poky communities like Zap, North Dakota, the village overwhelmed in last year's "zap-in." They reconstruct: through communes that make a simple product or provide a simple neighborhood service; through groups formed to speak, write, and work for ecology (stimulated at Columbia by the news that as a polluter of New York City air the university ranks fourth); or through efforts to make their employers give up antiquated ways, like the young insurgents in the State Department who caucused last year to protest its stagnation.

But whatever else they do, increasing numbers broadcast their protest by a different, a more natural, or a more beautiful personal style. Many young men recapture the hair fashions of their nineteenth-century forebears; the up-do of Andrew Jackson, the mane of Daniel Webster, the shoulder-length golden curls of General Custer—a prize Sitting Bull doted on.

So why wouldn't those who stay on campus press for more art? Press, that is, for the real thing, not for the pedantry of art history or the professionalism and commercialism of the concert halls and symphonies, the galleries and museums, or Broadway.

Students demand creative art because it is the most social of the academic disciplines. It counteracts the privacy of their other academic work. A student who writes up her analysis of the surface tension of a soap bubble, or another who reconstructs the geography of *Finnegans Wake*, works only for the attention of an instructor, who then responds with a few scribbles in the margin. It is scarcely plausible that students would read their course papers to friends for the pleasure of sharing the ideas. But they paint, act, compose, or dance for a number of others in the college community. They must display their work or perform it for an audience. Many fellow students enjoy it; some dislike it. In artistic creation, a personality converses freely with the world.

Robert Butman, Professor of Drama at Haverford College, believes that art can improve the teaching in other departments. Only 15 to 25 per cent of the Haverford faculty attend college plays, he estimates. "This is a pity, as in many cases professors get completely new ideas of a student's true abilities by watching him on the stage. This can lead to a better understanding between the two and a greater interest in each other—even in the course taught by the professor."

Students also want art as mind expansion, for that deeper knowledge that some think they can get only through drugs. Call it meaning. Most academic study now excludes meaning at any effective level. Says a sophomore studying philosophy: "My instructors consider it a scholar's game." A senior in engineering sums up: "Through all my four years only one of the faculty tried to relate his course to other subjects." Graduate study is no better. A student seeking an advanced degree in sociology notes: "We get methodology and theory galore, but the department despises social workers."

In turning to art, students are escaping this intellectual bankruptcy. The logic of art is expansive. Art abhors the barriers set up by specialists. It can help free the scholars. It can break the spell now keeping them from finding ideas needed to save our society. Beauty opened the eyes of Noble Laureate James Watson to the double helix as the key to heredity and life. The easy spiral described by the figure of the helix closely follows Hogarth's "line of beauty." With each more helical rearrangement of his model of the DNA molecule, Watson would exclaim, "It's so pretty it must be true!"

College students want creative art because its value is immediate. Most of them come from the middle class or are being groomed for it. They have been trained to the puritan ethic: work not for joy today but for salvation tomorrow. So they study their way through high school and college to amass credentials, always preparing themselves to survive a sorting out, whether for their education or their vocation. Getting in line for Judgment Day!

But in their art courses they do the work for the doing of it. Its value lies in the execution; judgment and reward are immediate; salvation comes not tomorrow but today when someone sees or hears what they've done and says, "Good."

Finally, students want art because it helps them find out who they are. One of the main functions of schools and colleges has always been to prevent that discovery. Fortunately, ever since the Babylonians, many of the younger generation have nevertheless sought it. Today, in reaction against the most massive academic and social system in history, the young are striving more vehemently than ever to identify themselves. No wonder they turn to art.

"You've got to think a lot about what's inside you before you dare show it to other people," warned a Columbia College sophomore. He was prowling around campus, movie camera in hand, starting on his term assignment in Film R402x, "The Documentary." I left him shooting an argument between some touch-football players and a gardener who was supposed to seed a patch of lawn they were churning into March mud.

What is the danger that the arts, like the other seminal disciplines before them, will be corrupted by the academicians? Instead of helping man grow greater, will they also be used to socialize an elite or drill a meritocracy? I believe not. I believe art will become academically domesticated without suffering the damage that befell the classics and the sciences. In all three disciplines, excellent work requires study, order, and no little pain. But art must also be approached as play. In the classics and in science, at the level where Erasmus or Einstein fulfilled himself, play is essential. But it is essential in art at the level where you and I come in. Art is too lively to be sanctified.

Instead, it can restore the balance in education between mind and spirit. It can enliven science with more wonder at the beauty of the universe. It can fire the humanities with more passion. It can wake the social and behavioral scientists from their nightmare in which society appears as a crushing juggernaut and let them see it as an absorbing tragicomedy. Art can draw the faculty away from their wizardry. It can give the students that gift for which King Solomon prayed—an understanding heart.

# 23 / *Survival*

*Horam expecta. Veniet.*
—On a campus sundial

The Columbia College daily paper in a recent historical article reported that our nineteenth-century-dean John Howard
Van Amringe interviewed students through an office boy. Apparently this did not turn them off. They loved him anyway.
In the East Quadrangle, alumni built a small round Roman
temple to shelter a bronze head of Van Amringe, his stern expression aggravated by a mustache whose ends reach well below
his chin. DEAN OF COLUMBIA MANY A DAY, reads the inscription.
THE LIGHT HE LEAVES BEHIND HIM LIES UPON THE PATHS OF
MEN.

Early this century, our president Nicholas Murray Butler was
a constructive and imaginative leader: he helped found the College Board when admissions were chaotic, he sponsored the first

modern General Education program, and he backed two experimental colleges. But a haughty attitude marked his long reign. He ran the university like a dictator and led the life of a sultan. He aped the industrial and financial leaders who supported him, even installing a mahogany-paneled private elevator to his office. The architecture of his administration building was imperial Roman, and, like an emperor, Butler peremptorily dismissed both radical students and liberal professors. We still suffer from the numbing effects of his authoritarianism. But the alumni from the days of this educational czar recall their college experience with nostalgia.

Since then, our faculty and administrative style has softened —somewhat. President McGill plays touch football and baseball Sunday afternoons with a noisy rabble of other administrators and students. A sophomore who works in our office challenged him and his staff to a snowball fight with us. Dr. McGill, who has a good arm, took care of himself nicely. Also, since the Bust, faculty and administrators have appeared more aware that students are people and that the university exists in a society. But all in all, Columbia is still an impersonal, a formidable, sometimes even an oppressive institution.

Yet in my opinion the best-educated young men in America come out of Columbia. A bold assertion? If true, why? I guess one reason is they've survived more. The challenges are heavier, the stimuli sharper. The words around our official seal flaunt this advantage: COLUMBIA UNIVERSITY IN THE CITY OF NEW YORK. That means the next person you pass may be a junkie or a Nobel Laureate; the next meal you eat out, a Chock Full o' Nuts hamburger or Japanese sukiyaki; the next student you talk to, a native of the Bronx, of Boise, or of Mali; the next sound you hear, the crooning of a pigeon or the boom of a jet out of Kennedy. You go to the football stadium by subway. If you keep a car, you park it on the street and move it every day to avoid accumulating fifteen-dollar parking tickets from the city police. Finding an off-campus apartment seems like winning in the state lottery. Two of my advisees have been mugged. One of them speculates that Columbia's student riots were more serious than Harvard's because New York's black Harlem is a more shocking contrast with a university than is white, lower-middle-class Cambridge. The guilt runs deeper here.

Also, Columbia educates her sons for independence. "This university leaves you alone, man. You're required to do only two things: show up for exams and not get caught with drugs." Many of the faculty are warm and helpful—when cornered. And the deans keep up the Open Door tradition established a generation ago by the famous Dean Herbert Hawkes, who was the first person a student encountered when he walked into the Dean's Office—but their building is now guarded by a formidable statue of alumnus Alexander Hamilton. He needed no help from his elders; rather, it was he whose impassioned speech saved Columbia's president Myles Cooper, a Tory, from a lynch mob of enthusiastic patriots. Facing out under the lindens toward Van Amringe's temple, Hamilton challenges the dean's avuncular frown with a theatrical posture of independence.

Nevertheless, Columbia College tries to offer undergraduates special help. The Dean's Office asks a group of sixty or seventy faculty and staff to try to establish rapport with undergraduates as their advisers. I am one of them. The students need help, and so do I.

# 24 / Alma Mater

*Religion and learning are justified of their children. To extend and intensify their elevating and twice-blessed power this college and university exist.*

—From a granite bench,
Columbia campus

Two suburbanites, two Brooklynites, two New Yorkers, two blacks, two Puerto Ricans, one California surfer, one Middle Westerner, two Yankees, three small-town boys, two Irish Catholics, two aristocrats, and a Jersey City football star. This is a list of those for whom I am or have been official adviser.

How are they doing?

The freshmen are into their second semester. They're all bored by a majority of their courses but inspired by at least one, usually because the teacher is wonderful. After his first day of classes, in one of which he was assigned to read Plato, the Puerto Rican declined to go out to drink beer. Instead he read the *Republic* through, finishing it in the small hours. "That cat Socrates had some fine things to say about Justice."

On a recent Saturday night, he also read through a draft of this book of mine. Did he like it? He liked it. In fact, he sat for an hour and a half Sunday morning thinking about his education.

Another has read very little of anything yet—his brother was killed in Vietnam a couple of days before college began, and his father was hospitalized in November with an incurable disease. Two appealed to me to recommend to them an elective for the spring term. I quoted the Dean of Freshmen, urging us to advise some of our students to take fliers. "Explore the catalogue," I urged. One chose Evolution of the Cities in anthropology; the other Introductory Tibetan. Still another ranked his first-year educational accomplishments as follows: number one, the Muhammad Ali-Joe Frazier fight; two, working as assistant manager of varsity basketball—seeing from the inside how those players handle themselves; three, learning how to pace college work; four, studying Erikson's *Young Man Luther* in two courses—in one for the politics, in the other for the psychology. "And, Mr. Gummere, that prof made us apply Erikson's psychology of developmental tasks to *ourselves*."

The sophomores are cool but busy. About half have found a major easily. One decided on Russian language and literature. Why? Because he sees himself as a superfluous man in the style of Chekhov. One methodical fellow picked his major by elimination, ticking off everything he did not want for any reason and arriving in the end at philosophy. "Do any employers want philosophy majors?" "Most don't care what you major in." One picked economics because he thinks it will help him make lots of money.

One sophomore asked if he could avoid majoring in anything. "Why must everybody my age specialize in an academic field? Do they want us all to be professional scholars?" "The faculty seem to," I warned him. I added that others have tried to be excused from a major without success. But I told him of a professor who proposed this past year to our faculty that they relieve any young generalist like him of this burden. And I consoled him with an account of the old-time college a century and a half ago where everybody studied all the same subjects all the time.

The juniors and seniors are officially out of their original advisers' hands and under their major departments. But most come back to talk anyway. One junior is a passionate scholar devouring political science, and lots else. He, too, read a draft of this book and said he liked it, especially the chapter on the Countercurriculum. But the book would have scared his parents. "Done 'em good, though." One junior is playing football and majoring in biology, another tennis and philosophy. "You know," said the philosopher, "I've figured out Plato. He was a frustrated dramatist. Missed his calling. The *Republic*, of course, is a spoof." Another got married, had a child, and dropped out.

The four juniors? Phil I've hardly seen in two years. He comes from someplace like Scranton, Pennsylvania. A friend told me he seems adjusted to fraternity life and to that academic jog of the final college years. The other three are restless, critical, distinctive. They've all wrestled with something formidable, as Jacob wrestled with the angel. And they've won, at least one bout. Joe came from near Youngstown, Ohio, recruited to play football. His face was handsome, juvenile, a little cherubic. He felt lost here. Too many ideas he could not grasp and people he could not enjoy. Halfway through his junior year, to the consternation of his parents, Joe withdrew, let his hair grow, and hit the road with a friend. They went South and West. After totaling their VW in California, Joe came East and worked three months on a Great Lakes freighter. He's back, finishing up, moderately interested in study. But he's passionately interested in a Buddhist sect, which he supports with all his best time and energy. The cherubic look is gone.

Nick is the son of a successful businessman whose home is in a fashionable suburb of New York. Sophomore year he angrily reported that the college wouldn't let him major in film, though an admissions officer had told him he could. I doubted that. But he was determined to transfer out anyway. He hated the required General Education program. Who wants to putter around a science lab? Who wants to read Augustine's *City of God*? But Nick is still here, majoring in English literature, which he chose on the following principle: "If you've gotta read a lot of books, they might as well be good ones." He has taken all the film courses allowed in our Graduate School of the Arts. He works on films part-time in an advertising agency. Summers he's made a documentary with a friend. He's found out how hard a good artist must work. "All that planning. Those hours and hours and hours of cutting, editing, cutting editing." He whistled at the recollection.

Sandy, another senior, has gone through college as an observer, finally majoring in sociology with a kind of condescension. He has been adroit at choosing courses; he does the unavoidable minimum of reading, and with the indulgence of faculty during our spring disturbances, he has managed to get to February of his senior year having written only one term paper.

But Sandy has been a conscientious student of the university. He's talked about its reform with the President and with most of the Deans. He was active in the moderate revolutionary organization Students for a Restructured University. He designed and proposed to the faculty an experimental cross-disciplinary course. Some of the best insights in this book I owe to him. Recently, Sandy says he's been "dropping acid."

The graduating seniors are already conducting themselves like young adults. I don't know about Carl, who after his freshman year transferred to Amherst and presumably is graduating there. How could he have known ahead that he wouldn't like this metropolitan university? Deep down, I think he may have felt our revolution of 1968 coming. He might have profited from it, like his classmate here who found he loved the college only after he saw it in terrible trouble. But Carl's wish for a more traditionally collegiate campus, as he put it, was understandable.

Anyway, transfers get and give more at their new college. They have better perspective. In his inaugural address President Kingman Brewster declared that he wanted to see more transfers, in and out of Yale. Ten years ago one of five entering students in our colleges was a transfer from another college. Since then, experts have estimated an even larger transfer figure.

Another graduating senior, Forbes, passed through Columbia

like a traditional collegian. He failed one course, enjoyed several hugely, and ignored the rest, getting through them at first with the study skills he'd acquired at a private school and then with the academic artifice that is the only practical benefit acquired by almost all graduates of American colleges. "Anyone bright enough to be admitted here can write a passable paper for any course in one afternoon—zing, zing, zing." Forbes put great discipline and intelligence into flying. I invited his parents to come and see me once when they were pressuring him into summer school to catch up academically and I was worried about the far worse pressure coming from an extraordinary crisis with his girl. His parents' generation, more casual in love as college students, hardly knew these upheavals. He met his with courage and grace.

Jeff was more of an intellectual than Forbes. He made me think of Pierre Bezukhov in *War and Peace*—big, awkward, but very personable. At one point he got interested in angels and hunted up every book in the place with information about angelology. I think he really believed in them. He told me he occasionally saw someone on the street who he believed was really an angel—incarnate. Here is Jeff's description of his decision on a career. His last summer he got a job on an oil rig in Wyoming. The other workers at first appalled him with their narrow, reactionary political and social ideology. Then he saw their decency to each other and to him. They were patient over his first mistakes with the heavy machinery. They asked him, a sophisticated Easterner, to their homes for a beer or a meal. After work Jeff would sit on the porch of his boarding-house in Powell, Wyoming, population 322, look out over the flat land, and think. Before leaving Powell, he decided to become a clergyman and serve in suburban communities, where people's humanity lies buried under a deeper layer of convention than the oil workers'.

Bob arrived a swashbuckling professional Californian, a man of the world already. You couldn't tell him anything. Within a few weeks, he concluded this was no place for him. He couldn't do the work, and couldn't stand the "intellectual hype." At first he planned to leave after a term or two. Then the college threatened to drop him anyway for academic failure. That led him to decide to make it, though I had to write two long letters to the Dean urging official patience.

Bob pledged at Beta, where the brothers, because they are college students still devoted to fun, seem like the Everglade kite, another species threatened with extinction. But in his sophomore year, he studied the European Balance of Power with Professor Herman Ausubel. Late one afternoon he stopped in and lectured me at length on the Italian Revolution. "Cavour was an aristocratic snob. He despised the peasant Garibaldi, who wanted to end the monarchy. But he saw that he might drive the Spanish Bourbons out of Italy. So Cavour practiced his exquisite patrician politicking in the capitals of Europe, and Garibaldi won the Italian Revolution in the field. 'Exquisite patrician politicking' are Professor Ausubel's words. The rest are mine." Bob says he now enjoys arguing politics with his father. "He's quite opinionated. But any time I want to, I can outargue him. Of course I do it very nicely."

The next summer some local young blacks, allegedly put up to it by the campus Left, broke into the Beta house and trashed it. On guard one hot night, with a shotgun across his knees, sick at the notion of even brandishing it, Bob got a message from a mobster for whom he'd worked as a waiter in an East Side bar: "If they come back, kid, phone us and we'll be right over; they'll never bother you again." Bob thought of Cavour and Garibaldi. If they could close the feudal gap, why not we and the blacks the racial gap? "Tell Louie no thanks. But tell him we're beholden to him. No, that just means he's real nice to want to help."

Of those seven of my advisees who were admitted in part as varsity athletic prospects, four soon decided not to play. The rest say they're glad they did. One whose high school football team was state champion says he learns more from being on our less successful one. The morale goes up throughout the season regardless of the record. A fencer says the most valuable thing he's learned at college is the principle instilled in him by the coach. "Remember, gentlemen, one touch at a time."

That coach, Irving Dekoff, was one of the most widely respected people at Columbia. Not only because his teams went undefeated for a five-year streak. Also, word got around that he was both sympathetic and strong. Sympathy isn't enough. A number of young people have shrugged off Charles Reich's book, *The Greening of America*. "Who needs a forty-year-old man to tell us our rejection of materialism is sound?" Instead, they want their elders to tell them the things they don't know. Like the oboe in a symphony orchestra tuning up, students give us the pitch. They give us our A. But after that, many of them seem to be looking for a strong conductor.

# 25 / Maestro

*How do you know what you do?*
—JAMES PERKINS
President of Cornell,
after his first drastic confrontation

A couple of years ago, when the youth revolution was going
strong, President N. Edd Miller, of the University of Nevada,
was called to campus early one morning. As he approached, he
saw a huge crowd of students. It looked like the whole university. He heard an uproar. Oh, no. Not here. He saw a large
sign. Picketing? We've blown it. They've occupied a building.
The shouting now sounded rhythmic. "We want Edd! We
want Edd!" He could read the words on the long banner:
N. EDD MILLER DAY. Fireworks began to go off.

The president flinched at the ROTC salute. And when he
got through the applauding crowd to the steps of the administration building and heard Jim Hardesty's speech, he had to
blink back some tears. But by the end of the morning, he could

take it better as they ushered him to lunch and he watched a thousand balloons float heavenward. And he had even grown calm by the time they presented him with the plaque, Mrs. Miller with the bracelet, and both with the tickets and hotel reservations and itinerary of a holiday in San Francisco.

He could now enjoy the formal but fervently spoken tribute: that he had coped with so many conflicting pressures—from conservatives and progressives, from students and faculty, from alumni and from state government; that he had not made the mistake of trying to please all parties; that throughout he had been honest with everybody.

After the speeches, President Miller began to feel wistful. How amateurish most of those decisions had seemed to him when they were made. How precarious the entente felt now. How many things had he not done for these young people. How soon, he asked himself, would they find him out? He sighed. "Someday they'll surely see through me." "Sir?" The one next to him leaned over to hear better. "Oh, nothing. I was just talking to myself. Delicious lunch, wasn't it? Our usual superb cuisine!"

# Afterword

*The opposite of a correct statement is a false statement. But the opposite of a profound truth may well be another profound truth.* —NIELS BOHR

I think I know why professors at liberal arts colleges condemn graduate schools of education with an intensity that is sometimes venomous. They feel seriously threatened by scholars who attempt seriously to study the processes of higher education. The educationists might someday communicate to a wide public what it is the academicians are doing.

Ten years ago, I studied higher education at Teachers College of Columbia University. At TC the faculty and students tried to acquire not some convenient overview of the nation's colleges and universities but a sense of their baffling, exciting complexity. Professor W. Max Wise, after a leave in which he investigated about eighty of them at some depth, returned and summed up what he had learned, with the sigh of a happy explorer: "It's a jungle."

At Teachers College I took a course offered by Dr. Wise: "The American College Student and His College." Be skeptical, he warned. Avoid sweeping statements about education. Pay very close attention to the life on your own campus. Interpret it boldly. Then and only then dare to generalize.

That is how I wrote this book. Is my story of higher education therefore too crowded with Easterners, especially with Columbia students? I'm convinced not. I'm convinced that their experience is representative. In all parts of the country, in all types of colleges or universities, I gather the institutional and human drama I've written about is being played. Only its pace varies. One purpose of the American college, now as always, is to get young people away from their family, out of their neighborhood, into a more sophisticated environment. Often this heightens the revolt they should be going through in those years anyway. Another purpose is to socialize them to fit the culture of the day. This can provoke many to even sharper revolt. An educator on a college campus must further both purposes no matter how sharply they clash. He therefore is caught in a dilemma as painful as it is old. But he can console himself with the thought that the reconciling of liberty and order is the epic task of man.

Only a genius, a Dewey, can write conclusively about education. Others should attempt less, and I have tried mainly to describe the latent functions, as the sociologists call them, of the American college. Because undeclared, you know these are the core functions of the system. In most times, it is better not to discuss them. Today, many of us feel ready to examine the core. And I think we must do it with the help of philosophers and experts, but also in the light of the Comic Spirit. If we shine that light often enough on higher education, everybody may get more out of it and enjoy it more.